To Robin, on his 49th ...
wishes

THE HARMONY OF THE HUM.

Armin J. Husemann, MD, born in 1950, is a general practitioner and head of the Anthroposophical Medical College at the Filder Clinic in Filderstadt, near Stuttgart. He lectures in a number of colleges in Germany and elsewhere.

To my father,
who was also my teacher,
in gratitude

Armin J Husemann

The Harmony of
the Human Body

Musical Principles in Human Physiology

Floris Books

Translated by Christian von Arnim
Part IV translated by Alan Stott

First published in German under the title
Der musikalische Bau des Menschen
by Verlag Freies Geistesleben, second edition in 1989.
This version, abridge by the author, first
published in English in 1994 by Floris Books.
Paperback reprint 2002.

British Library CIP Data available

ISBN 0-86315-380-1

Printed in Great Britain
by IBT Global, Barking

Contents

Acknowledgments

This translation would not have been possible without the generous support of the research department of the Association of Free Waldorf Schools, the Society of Anthroposophical Doctors as well as a number of readers of the German edition.

My thanks to the following for their kind permission to reproduce illustrations from their publications: Deutscher Taschenbuch Verlag (Figure 70); Schattauer Verlag (Figures 49 and 55); Springer Verlag (Figures 19, 44, 47, 52, 57, 76, 79, 83 and 87); Georg Thieme Verlag (Figures 1, 2, 3, 11a, 11b, 16, 66a, 66b, 67a, 67b); Urban und Schwarzenberg (Figures 27, 56, 84, 85, 86 and 88).

Preface

Since the first German appearance of this book, work on its subject-matter, the study of the human being from a sculptural, musical and linguistic perspective, has continued in the form of regular courses at two educational centres. The present revised and expanded edition is the result of my joint work with the artists and lecturers who teach there.*

The purpose of revising the book was to give greater clarity to the content of the first edition and to create a greater sense of unity, including some new, additional chapters. This has given the present edition a cohesion lacking in the earlier one. It results from working with the three modelling exercises which Rudolf Steiner gave to doctors and scientists in order to help them to train their understanding of the life processes on an Imaginative level. The exercises form the basis of the greater part of this book.

This work would not have been written without my father, Dr Gisbert Husemann, who was the first to put these guidelines by Rudolf Steiner into practice. Participation at the 'Working Weeks for the Study of the Human Being through Art' gave me the opportunity to become familiar with this way of working. In order to round off the book, some of the material from the 'Working Week for the Study of the Human Being through Art' 1975 (Stuttgart) has been reproduced here in freely expanded form. I wish to express my gratitude to the lecturers concerned, Gisbert Husemann, Wilfried Hammacher and Maria Schüppel, for giving their permission to publish the extracts here.

Warm thanks are due to my brother Dr Friedwart Husemann for his invaluable help and advice in checking the manuscript, and to Daniel

* Representative names are Frimut Husemann (sculpture), Felix Lindenmeier (music) and Dr Heinz Zimmermann (language) at the Rudolf Steiner Teacher Training Seminar in Dornach, Switzerland, as well as Manfred Welzel (sculpture) at the Christian Community Seminary in Stuttgart, Germany.

Moreau for his drawings. Furthermore, I am indebted to Dr Hans Müller-Wiedemann as well as the community of the Brachenreuthe special school for their understanding support of the work on this book. I owe thanks, too, to the Rudolf Steiner Research Fund, without whose support this book would not have been possible in its present form. I am also grateful to Walter Schneider and Jean-Claude Lin from the publisher, Verlag Freies Geistesleben, for their constructive co-operation.

Stuttgart, March 1989

Armin J. Husemann, M D

Introduction

Art and supersensory knowledge

Ever since anthroposophy began to play a role in the modern world,
it has been confronted with the following objection:

> Even if one accepts that Rudolf Steiner was able to conduct
> supersensory research, it is impossible for non-initiates to
> test the accuracy of the knowledge he has acquired in the
> 'higher worlds.' Anthroposophists are fond of talking about
> a 'scientific attitude,' but on closer examination their
> relationship to Steiner's teachings often bears more of a
> resemblance to medieval faith which accepts his works as a
> kind of revelation.

It is a compelling argument. After all, can I see the 'etheric body' or
the 'astral body' as described by Rudolf Steiner? For most people
today the answer will be no. How, then, can I justify practising as
a doctor or a teacher on the basis of information by Steiner in
which these higher elements of the human being play an essential
part?

It is difficult to refute this objection if we restrict ourselves to what
are commonly accepted criteria about the nature of knowledge. For
centuries natural science has nurtured an attitude which says that the
concept of knowledge in any rigorous scientific sense can only be
applied outwardly to the world of objects. Any investigation of the
self is immediately subjective and thus useless for scientific research.
The perspective of the observer when looking at the self is useless as
far as scientific knowledge is concerned.

But if we take into account that every statement about the nature of
'science' or 'knowledge' presupposes thinking activity, it follows that
the acknowledged division of the totality of human experience into

'subject' and 'object' is a product of the thinking. With reference to this, Rudolf Steiner concludes:

> Thinking is *beyond* subject and object. It produces these two concepts just as it produces all others. Therefore, when we as thinking subject refer a concept to an object, we must not regard this reference as a merely subjective activity. It not the subject that makes the reference, it is thinking. The subject does not think because it is a subject; rather it appears to itself as subject because it can think. Thus the activity the human being performs as a *thinking* being is not merely subject, neither is it objective; it transcends both concepts. I ought never to say that my individual subject thinks, for only by the grace of thinking does it exist as subject. Thus thinking is an element that takes me beyond myself and unites me with the objects. But at the same time it also separates me from them, placing me as a subject over against them.[1]

With this reflection on the nature of thinking Rudolf Steiner made it possible for the subject to be seen as a part of reality, which thereby becomes just as accessible to scientific research as the world of objects. To achieve this, the thinking has to understand itself as reality which can be justified on its own terms and can thus shake off the illusion of its 'subjectivity.' When it does that, it can confront the 'subject' in the same way as it does the 'object.' 'Subject' and 'object' become the concepts with which the thinking distinguishes its two fields of observation. By liberating the thinking in this way, Rudolf Steiner became the founder of a science of self-knowledge. 'On the basis of scientific method' the results of his observation of the soul led to the 'philosophy of freedom' while his spiritual observations led to 'anthroposophy.'

Returning to the objection which was voiced at the beginning, we can now respond that it is certainly true that outside myself I cannot generally see the etheric or astral body of another person. But my own being has to be made up of the same elements. I have quite different opportunities to observe my own etheric and astral bodies and my 'I' because I live in them. That part of my being which is not accessible to clear observation is described as 'unconscious.' The higher elements of my being therefore belong to the sphere of the subconscious. But is it not possible through the practice of art to raise experiences of the unconscious to consciousness, which in themselves allow us to recognize the kind of structures which Rudolf Steiner was describing? What do we experience in the act of sculpting, when we create music and language? What is it that moulds matter through my hands, what makes us phrase a piece of music in a certain way? Where does the shape of a 'diminuendo' come from, what gives a rest its meaning?

A new perspective give us the answers to these questions. The higher elements mentioned above shape the physical body at the embryonic stage. They leave the marks of their generative characteristics in the shape and function of the organs in the same way that a seal leaves its mark in sealing wax. The three-dimensional forms of the organs are produced through the activity of the etheric body which subordinates the autonomous structure of mineral substance in order to integrate it into its own living context. The more the activity of the organs is subject to and influenced by the consciousness, the more this is the result of the generative action of the astral body, which develops the senses, nerves and so on. It penetrates the etheric body to the varying degree with which the adult can consciously control his organs. The possibility of ego-consciousness in the ensouled and physically alive organism — leading to upright posture, speech and thinking — is due to the action of the ego-functions at the embryonic stage.[2]

This leads to the question of what happens to these powerful organic generative forces when the organs have developed and assumed their final shape? A part of them will always remain linked with the organs in the regenerative and functional metabolism. But the rest becomes surplus to requirement, otherwise the organism would continue to develop and grow. It is these surplus generative forces which appear in the consciousness as creative artistic forces in painting, sculpture and so on, on the one hand, and as conceptualizing powers on the other. What human beings no longer need for their bodies turns into the capacity to give meaning to the world through art, science and social interaction; it creates human culture. There is therefore a close correlation between the organic development of the child and the development of his creative thinking and artistic powers. Anthroposophical education and medicine are based on Rudolf Steiner's detailed investigation of the ages at which specific generative forces become surplus in the organism and are thus made available for emotional and intellectual development.

Thus through sculpting, the unconscious generative forces of the etheric body which underlie our organic development make their appearance in our consciousness as an experience of the will. But this has the indeterminate, mysterious character of every uncomprehended perception. With Goethe's methodology the life of three-dimensional surfaces becomes comprehensible as a living idea, as the archetype which metamorphoses from one form into another. If we understand the living idea underlying the organism, we have taken the first conscious step to understanding its life. Knowledge in this form can lead to an Imaginative understanding of the etheric body. But the first thing is to emphasize that the archetype of the organism is its etheric body as reflected in the living idea. This is how Rudolf Steiner described the etheric body in his presentation of the threefold structure of the human being.[3] The etheric body is represented there in the threefold archetype of the physical body.

The experiences of the sculptor thus find their conceptual counterpart in a Goethean way of thinking. Steiner therefore set modelling exercises for the study of the etheric body in which the organs can be understood as metamorphosing one from the other, based on archetypal forms in a Goethean sense. When the artist's world of three-dimensional experience combines in this way with Goethe's living perception of ideas, we have the beginnings in the will of our own perception of the etheric body.

The superfluous generative impulses of the astral body metamorphose to a greater or lesser degree into musical creativity. The liberated generative forces of the 'I' come 'to expression' in language. The latter's ego-like unity in the formation of musical vowels and sculpted consonants turns into physical sound. The practical investigation of the human constituent elements through a study of the human being in sculpture, music and language raises the scientific study of the physical body to the level of a comprehensive science of the whole human being. It is achieved in four stages:

1. Anatomy of the physical body.
2. Sculpting the organs according to specially given basic or archetypal forms in a Goethean sense in order to achieve understanding of the etheric body.
3. Musical studies from a number of perspectives, such as the study of proportions in a Pythagorean sense, to investigate the astral body.
4. Study of language based on the phenomenology of speech sounds, grammar as well as anthroposophical speech formation and dramatic art.

By this means it is possible to verify Steiner's supersensory findings in areas where ordinary consciousness today has the capacity to observe them: in the deeper strata of a person's own being, brought to consciousness through artistic exercise.

The combination of such artistic perceptions with Goethean concepts, as developed further by Steiner, brings about an independent understanding of the higher elements in the human being in their embryonic forms. The latter are open to future development: into Imagination at the modelling stage, Inspiration at the musical stage and Intuition at the language stage of the path.

PART I

The Outer Pictorial Nature of the Human Being

1. The sculptural conception of organs

At first sight, the three-dimensional forms of the human body appear at rest like the forms of a sculpture. But an internal, scientific view of the vital processes teaches us that every organ with its spatial contours is subject to degenerative forces which are not immediately visible, balanced by a simultaneous process of regeneration. The relevant form lives in a floating equilibrium which can be compared to a stationary wave in a river. Nevertheless, in the course of our lives 'equilibrium' in the real sense of the word only exists for a passing phase. In the infant the generative processes predominate; in the middle years there is equilibrium; and in old age degeneration takes over. The generative processes in the infant create the convex forms of the head, the cheeks, the back of the hands and the feet. In mid-life these shapes have stretched and in old age concave surfaces and wrinkled lines dominate the picture. They are the three-dimensional expression of the degenerative forces.

We can illustrate what underlies these changes in shape during life by a comparison of the patterns of sleeping and waking in children and the elderly. At first, the newborn baby is awake only for a few hours per day. From six to twelve months the child still sleeps up to eighteen hours daily. In adulthood this has been reduced to an average of eight hours. In old age five to six hours of sleep are often sufficient. The length of time that we stay awake therefore increases in the course of our life. Wakefulness depends on the functions of the sensory and nervous systems, whose degenerative activity also results in tiredness. In the absence of sensory and nervous activity during sleep the generative processes predominate. Thus the sculptural transformation of the body becomes linked with the growing length of time that we remain awake during life: increasing sensory and nervous activity promotes the degenerative processes which gradually turn the convex forms into concave ones.

A comparison of plants and animals emphasises this polarity even more clearly. Plants lack the sensory and nervous systems found in animals and thus the physical basis for wakefulness. Although what are described as 'sensory organs' in plants mediate between the plant and its environment (light, touch, etc.), they do not create conscious sensations in the plant. It therefore lives wholly in the generative processes. Once its forms have come into existence, it cannot reduce them again degeneratively in order to transform them into something new. Once they have been created they remain in existence. The cotyledons are often still visible when blossoming starts. With animals, in contrast, embryonic forms are subject to change until the organs reach their final state of development. Sections of tissue migrate and flow. Plant cells in principle remain immobile at the place where they originated after cell division. Here, on a cellular level, we can see immobility as the characteristic quality of plants, contrasted with animal mobility.

Surface curvature in plants comes about through the varying degrees to which the cells extend their growth. On the concave lower surface of the leaf this archetypal degenerative shape becomes evident only as a reduced intensity of growth. At the first invagination, or infolding, of the animal embryo during gastrulation, there is a clear inward migration of cells. The archetypal action which occurs with gastrulation in the formation of the archenteron, or primitive gut, and thus of the first bodily cavity, is repeated as the decisive sculptural formative action in the development of all animal organic systems.

The nervous system is formed through the invagination of the neural tube; in the metabolic system the pleuroperitoneal cavity is also created through invagination; and the respiratory system arises through

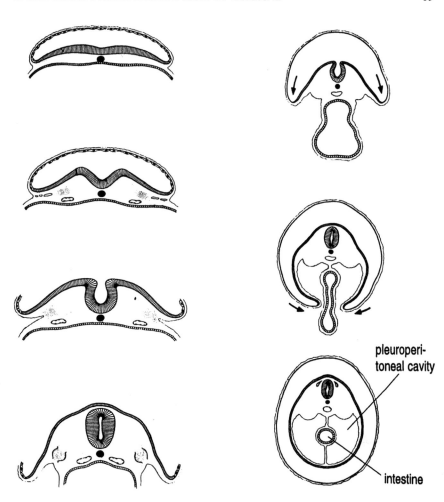

Figure 1. Formation of the
neural tube.

Figure 2. Formation of the pleuroperitoneal cavity and the intestine.

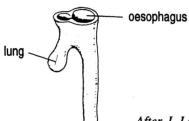

Figure 3.
Formation of the lung.

After J. Langman,
Medizinische Embryologie

the invagination of the anterior wall of the primitive gut to form the lung.

The development of increasingly concave surfaces from infancy to old age through the influence of the sensory and nervous systems is thus shown also to be the basic pattern of animal embryonic development, in contrast to that of the plant. With the pattern of invagination we have grasped a type of sculptural formative action which transforms predominantly vegetative and generative organizational stages into such ones which develop the organs of feeling and waking consciousness. This independence of the sculptural archetype from its physical substrate, in other words from the genetic pattern present in the tissue, can be immediately understood from the theory of knowledge which Steiner developed for organic science.

This independence has also been substantiated experimentally. Invagination, for instance, was observed not only with the inward migration of cells as in gastrulation, but

> even in unfertilized eggs a 'pseudo-blastopore' will form
> within two to three days of treatment with progesterone, that
> is, without previous cell division. The progesterone clearly
> provokes an acceleration of development so that this
> gastrulation-like movement occurs in the wrong place of the
> developmental process.'[4]

In the same way that invagination is typical for feeling organisms,[5] outwardly orientated convex expansion is the archetypal movement of the largely sleeplike vegetative life which finds its purest form of expression in the plant. In summary we have the scheme opposite.

This polarity has been thoroughly investigated and described by, among others, O. Hertwig, Th. Goebel, G. Wachsmuth, G. Zickwolf.[6] W. Schad describes one example of the interaction of plant and animal from a sculptural and musical perspective:

> The plant world, too, can make sounds, but not on its own.
> It is made to sway and rustle in the wind. ... In the East
> African steppes there is even a type of acacia, *Acacia seyal,*
> whose round and bloated leaf stems produces a sound after
> certain types of ant first drill holes into the wooden bubbles
> in which they then proceed to live. The plant cannot
> produce its flute-like tones on its own.[7]

	Plants	*Animals*
Embryology, morphogenesis	Immobile cells; earlier stages are preserved	Cell migration and mobility; earlier stages are broken down and transformed
Life process	Generative	Generative and degenerative
Dominant state of consciousness	Sleeping	Waking
Process-equivalent human stage	Infancy	Old age
Three-dimensional developmental motion	Expansion	Invagination

The three-dimensionality of organs thus reveals the predominance of etheric, living forces in expansion; the action of the astral body, on the other hand, can be seen in invagination. The following chapters will be concerned with establishing how the sculptural expression of the human etheric body can be perceived. Not only is it permeated by a sentient body, but it is also transformed into an instrument of the self-conscious 'I.' The two types of movement mentioned so far, expansion and invagination, are therefore supplemented by a third one, inversion, which will have to be examined in detail.

2. The sculptural action of the etheric body

Rudolf Steiner set out a number of modelling exercises which are designed to transform the living perception of ideas, as described in the previous chapter, into the Imaginative perception of the etheric body. We will begin by describing an exercise which can show how the outer human form results from the activity of the etheric body. This will be followed by the relevant exercise for the inner organs.

We take as much clay, plasticine or wax as can be comfortably held in the hand. Then we form it into a sphere. This sphere is not created through inherent characteristics of the material, but through the movement of our arms, hands and fingers. Blood flows through the arteries in our arms into the fingers. The activity of the blood is transformed into muscular motion which forms the material. The more we slow down the movement of our hands and fingers while we are modelling, the more we become aware of the life of the etheric body in these movements. Moving at a speed which corresponds approximately to the motion of the chest during relaxed breathing has shown itself to be effective. An equilibrium arises between the sense of touch in our fingertips and the experience of the will in the action of the muscles. In this way our feeling can immerse itself in the sculptural activity of the etheric body.

Attention to time is an important factor in any investigation of the etheric. Hand movements which are too rapid come too close to the speed of thinking in the nervous system and lose their vitality. People today who do not have any artistic experience of modelling have to make a conscious effort to put themselves in a phlegmatic mood.

In imagining a sphere, Rudolf Steiner suggests an image taken from nature, the droplet, as a reflection of the totality of the cosmic environment. The latter is reflected in its purest form in the shape of the human head.

Now think of the droplet as being extended into a cylinder.

If you do this while imagining that the elements from the

cosmos which have taken shape in the head remain, except that they are modified in all kinds of ways through extending the droplet into a cylinder, you are left with the human torso.

When looking at the torso we have to think of the calvaria as having atrophied. But then, having created the cylinder and indented it here, you have to think of this as the third stage. This leaves you with the limbs; what I have drawn here will initially be reflected in the arms. Thus you have to imagine an extension which in the first instance turns into the arms. A second extension is formed by the creation from within of another image which stems from the moon. But ignore the arms in order not to complicate matters. Thus we start with the sphere, elongate it and progress from there to invagination. ... So think of a sphere which has been elongated; that is the upward extension caused by the environment. If you think of the earth with its forces here in contrasting terms to the environment, you have the earth below the human being as the infolding force.[8]

In our morphological examination of Chapter 1, we recognized the infolding formative motion as a result of the activity of the astral body. Above, Rudolf Steiner refers to the forces of the earth as the cause of invagination. That is no contradiction. The soul elements which are incarnated in the physical matter of a living organism in themselves have no spatial dimension. As expressions of the soul (that is, separately from their content) neither will impulses nor sensations nor thoughts have any spatial qualities. If this non-spatial nature of the astral body wishes to be incarnated in etheric and in physical matter, it has to combine with one of those two forces. But the conscious sentient life is linked with the degeneration of life forces. It comes to expression when what is alive enters the process of returning to its dead mineral state: in the nerves. With that we have touched upon the riddle of the link between the soul and the body. The soul can only experience itself in the body by resisting the life of the latter. The sentient body is allied to the mineral forces radiating from the earth which are active in the degenerative process. We will

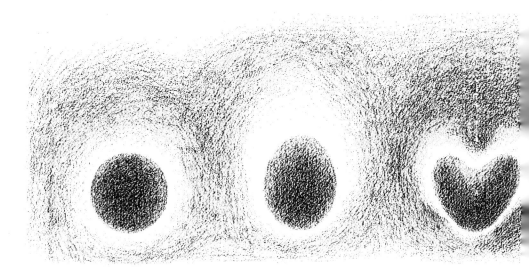

Figure 4. Modelling exercise by Rudolf Steiner. Drawings by Daniel Moreau.

expand this image of the astral body further when we consider its musical nature.

The extent to which the range of forms in Figure 4 corresponds to Rudolf Steiner's information will become clear below in a number of ways. In the final, fifth form the sculptural formative action coincides with the form of the physical body. It shows the alignment of the human form as it is usually found in the waters of the womb. It is thus in the same alignment as the plant, with the mineral pole turned towards the earth and the life pole towards the environment. This alignment also corresponds to the etheric element in the human being for as long as the astral body and the 'I' have not become active in the etheric and physical body in a conscious way. With birth and the first intake of breath the intervention of the astral body turns the form so that the spine is aligned parallel to the earth's surface. The 'I' brings about a further ninety degree rotation. This gives us an overview of the way that the position of the physical body is determined by the higher elements in the human being. (Figure 5).

The purpose of this modelling exercise as an image of evolution is made clear in the description by the science of the spirit of the head as the 'oldest limb,' the chest as a more recent one and the limbs as

the most recently created organs.[9] The evidence for this is supplied, in turn, by natural science through the basic law of biogenesis (see page 54) according to which (in Goethean terms) embryonic development reflects an abbreviated recapitulation of our evolutionary development in general. Here too, and in the subsequent period of growth, the head, torso and limbs develop consecutively.

Figure 6 illustrates the different growth stages of the human being. In order to give a clearer comparison of the proportions, they have been adjusted to a uniform size.[10] Looked at from the perspective of

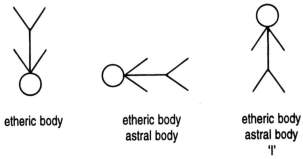

etheric body   etheric body   etheric body
                      astral body   astral body
                                                'I'

Figure 5.

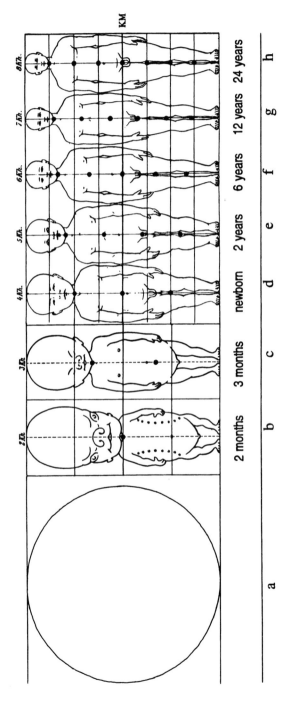

Figure 6. The changing proportions in the growing human being (from Stratz et al.)

the modelling exercises, this series can be interpreted as substance increasingly flowing from the head into the limbs. The head retains its original shape, but it 'shrinks' as it were. From a functional perspective the human form becomes polarized: the head is deprived of life which moves to the metabolic and limb systems. The brain, which is incapable of regeneration, has as its polar opposite the reproductive forces in the lower body. From the time of birth, the head grows to twice its size, the arms by a factor of three, the torso four and the legs to five times their size.[11] Thus the real direction of growth in the human being is from the top downwards, as illustrated in Figure 7.

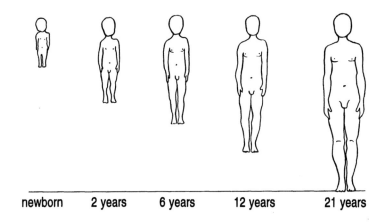

| newborn | 2 years | 6 years | 12 years | 21 years |

Figure 7.

If we supplement this representation of three-dimensional growth with results gained from the observation of children, we can say that the human being to begin with consists of nothing but 'head.' Then changes take place in such a total 'head-being' which enable it to set foot on earth. To indicate this we have added *a* to Stratz's depictions in Figure 6 to represent the archetypal sphere. The question whether there is any justification for this archetypal sphere encompasses the issue of what happens with conception in the etheric organization of the human being. (This will be dealt with in greater detail in the Chapter 13 on the musical physiology of reproduction.) The sphere is the archetypal shape of the prenatal spiritual embryo of the human being which has its physical correlation in the maternal egg cell. From the microscopic size of ordinary body cells the egg cell expands during its development in the ovaries into a sphere which becomes the largest cell in the body. The spiritual embryo of the infant self, with its developmental prescriptions from earlier lives, unites with this form. From the father the embryo receives the power to sculpt the rest of the body from this sphere, to add the physical body to the head.

> The point is that fertilization essentially only affects the limb system, everything which is not head. For the head of the human being is essential shaped not by the male but by the whole of the cosmos. The head of the human being is not conceived from the male but from the cosmos. The head is already predisposed in the unfertilized egg ... so that we can discover even from the physical study of human embryological development, if it is done properly, that the head develops out of the body of the mother before there is any input from fertilizing forces ...[12]

When we model a sphere we create a three-dimensional image of the head in potential, which has its physical equivalent in the female germ cell. Fertilization by the father thus takes place in between the spherical stage, representing the head in its totality (Figure 6, *a*), and its subsequent expansion (Figure 6, *b*). That is the reason for preceding the embryo with the archetypal sphere, the equivalent of the human being before conception, at twice the size of the head. In that initial sphere the Imaginative series of shapes in the modelling exercises coincides with our understanding of embryological development.

Through this modelling exercise the thinking gains the capacity to grasp phylogenesis as explained by spiritual science, ontogenesis as observed in embryology and the development of functional organic differentiation as an expression of a single sculptural formative stream and its rhythm. Spiritual ideas start to become evident in the physical body. In this way the thinking creates the framework for an understanding of the active forces which have to be taken into account with conception in relation to the child. The social understanding of what is happening as human beings attempt to incarnate, which is so urgently necessary at present, assumes this kind of sculpturally vitalized thinking in the training of doctors.

3. Blood flow and etheric flow

The question which the modelling exercise sought to answer from the perspective of the science of the spirit was related to the 'fluid constitution' of the human being. The etheric body lives above all in the blood and in the fluids which are connected with the blood. That is why the flow of the blood even in the mature human being still shows up the motion with which the etheric body produced the outer human shape. The blood which works to regenerate the body flows into the limbs in an expansive movement. The motion of invagination is characteristic of the blood which carries the waste products from the limbs. The arterial quality of the blood has its origins in the cosmic environment which renegerates the blood with the intake of breath. 'Inhalation is caused by the cosmos whereas the earth causes exhalation. The cosmos gives us pure oxygen whereas the earth causes the latter to be impregnated with carbon, thus producing the devitalizing air we exhale' (Steiner[13]). The venous quality of the blood becomes evident in the exhalation of carbon dioxide, the last stage in the degenerative process.

As sound, such air becomes the vehicle of emotional and intellectual expression in song and language. When we referred earlier to the non-spatial character of the astral, the purely negative definition of this concept is here filled with content. The quality of that power in the human being, which can only express itself negatively in the living physical body as a degenerative, life-destroying force, is revealed as the non-spatial, imageless quality of music.

Thus two opposing streams interpenetrate in the human being — a sculptural generative stream in the physical vehicle of the arterial blood and a musical stream which is embodied in the venous blood as the vehicle of degenerative processes. The 'I' uses the sculptural stream when we move and act, the musical stream when we sing, speak and think. (The extent to which in reality both streams intermingle with one another in numerous ways will become clear later on. Here we only refer to their basic qualities.)

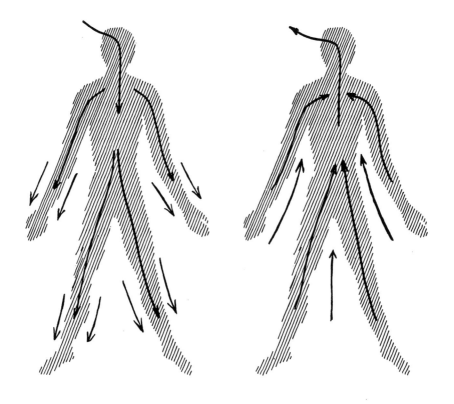

Figure 8. Plastic stream   *Musical stream*

The flow of the etheric body represented in the motion of the blood is repeated in the fundamental polarity of limb movement. Extension is the activity of the etheric body in the finished physical body which is equivalent to the expansion it promoted during growth. The activity of invagination continues functionally when we bend. Extension and flexion are described in the following way in eurythmy:

> Every time that we stretch something of the will leaves us and the aura which surrounds us brightens somewhat. My action continues beyond me. Movements with a rod have the same effect. The aura is consciously extended. We can also throw the rod. The rod can be replaced by a bud or the branch of a fir-tree whose twigs have been tied together. Extension carries the will beyond the person, releases

vitality. ... Flexion takes external forces from the aura and
internalizes them. The surrounding aura is darkened. Flexion
consumes inner vitality; the forces of the aura streaming in
from the outside consume the human being. The latter will
burn up inside if he does nothing but flex. Bending, the
internalization of the aura, corresponds to taking hold of
something which is alive such as a branch or a forked stick
(Steiner[14]).

The modelling exercises make it directly clear why extension can be
Imaginatively elucidated by throwing a bud, whereas flexion is
elucidated by receiving a forked stick. Hegel already wrote in his
philosophy of nature:

The difference between the arterial and the venous blood
becomes reality in the lung and the liver; it is the contrast
between the extensor and the flexor. Arterial blood
represents outgoing, dispersive activity, venous blood
inward contraction ...[15]

In one respect, the view that the flow of the blood copies the
etheric motion which modelled the physical body appears to contain
a contradiction. For while we think of the plastic stream as radiating
from the head downwards, the arterial blood in the carotid artery
which is subordinated to this motion flows in the opposite direction.
Here it becomes clear that the complex processes of the organism
cannot be expressed in a single image. Two opposing formative
principles do indeed interpenetrate one another in the head to the
extent that the sphere to which we referred earlier is the result of
inversion. We will consider this plastic formative principle in detail in
Chapter 18; then something which still appears as a contradiction at
this point will turn out to represent the living essence of the case.

4. The musical physiology
of blood circulation and respiration

Respiration represents the inner motion which exists in the transformation of venous blood into arterial blood. With this we have left the fluid part of the human being for the respiratory activity of the astral body. That, as we explained in the introduction, entails the transition to a musical perspective.

Extension reflects in the motion of the limbs that which is represented as inner quality in the arterial blood. It is experienced on a soul level as outwardly directed excess vitality. In flexion, the limbs copy the motion of the venous blood as it contracts to the centre. Human beings experience this on a soul level as the absorption of outside influences which repress their own vitality. That contrast is experienced musically in the major and minor moods.

The following melodic phrase by Mozart develops the mood which is set up with the major third around the opening note B. The soul spreads its wings.

Example 1.

The minor version of the same phrase might sound as follows if it were schematically transposed.

Example 2.

The effect is empty and lacks conviction. The reason for this becomes clear when it is compared with Mozart's variation on the theme in the minor key.

Example 3.

With the minor third the soul turns inward and becomes more reflective. And if this melody is to find a convincing answer to the opening one it has to incorporate the spirit of the minor mood in the same way that the first melody is in accord with the major key. They present a penetrating example of the way that 'beauty' lies in the revelation of the inner law.

To sum up:

extension <—— *physical motion* ——> flexion

expansion <—— *sculptural motion* ——> invagination
in etheric body

major <—— *musical motion* ——> minor
in astral body

Mourning over the death of a person is a fundamental experience of the soul. The motion with which the body is carried in a funeral procession introduces the 'minor' mood into the soul with the same necessity that the venous blood is projected into our musical experience as the minor mood. For in the venous blood the body of the continuously dying human being is 'carried to the grave.' A funeral march in a major key would be impossible because it would contradict the musical physiology of the blood.

Suffering causes us to breath in more deeply — the sob when we cry. The joy which makes human beings more extrovert increases exhalation in laughter. A cheerful character will constitutionally incline to greater exhalation while a more serious, melancholy one will do so towards inhalation:

> To begin with I want to say a few words about the relationship of the major to the minor key. If we want to understand the more intimate aspects of music we have to develop an awareness of the way in which music corresponds to subtle structures in the human being. In other words, what comes to expression in music responds in a certain way to the subtle inner constitution of human beings.[16]

Steiner then describes the way in which within such subtle structural comparisons a difference can be noted between people who have a preference for inhaling — he calls them 'oxygen freaks' — and others whose inner constitution is particularly prone to the pushing-away of exhalation. The former constitution forms the basis for the melancholic temperament while the latter does so for the sanguine one. It is obvious from this that the soul element is tied more closely to the body when we breath in — the first breath of the newborn baby is to inhale — whereas when we exhale there is greater severance of the soul from the physical and etheric body. The final breath of the deceased is to exhale. If we understand the lung on the basis of the sculptural invagination of the astral body into the physical and etheric body it follows that the functional continuation of that infolding motion, inhalation, also receives its impulse from the astral body. That is confirmed by the research of spiritual science. Steiner continues his explanation:

> We breath in with the astral body and we expel the air again with the etheric body. ... The contrast between these different human temperaments is linked to the origin of the major and minor scales in the sense that everything which is an experience of the minor mood is based ... on that human constitution which lusts for oxygen, which experiences with a certain pleasure the astral body striking against the etheric one. The major scales, in contrast, are based on the feelings of pleasure when the etheric body in turn strikes the astral, or the feeling of being uplifted, of relief, of zest when that happens.

Looked at in terms of the processes involved, the two motions connected with the major mood, the exhalation of the lungs and the arterial flow of the blood, are in accord with one another. Both are part of an expansive motion in which the 'etheric body in turn striking the astral' is experienced. In the same way inhaling and the diastolic flow of the venous blood can be seen as two metamorphoses of a single comprehensive invaginative motion. But a contradiction arises when these processes are looked at from the qualities governing the blood. The diastolic flow of the venous blood experienced in the minor mood extends physiologically into the major mood of breathing out; and the minor mood of breathing in contains the regenerative forces for the major mood of the arterial blood. This contradiction rests on the fact that we have so far observed two processes without taking account of their living organic link. After all, the peripheral circulation does not enter the lung directly. We have failed to take the heart into account.

The venous blood concludes the process of internalization in the right ventricle of the heart. There the blood accumulates back on itself

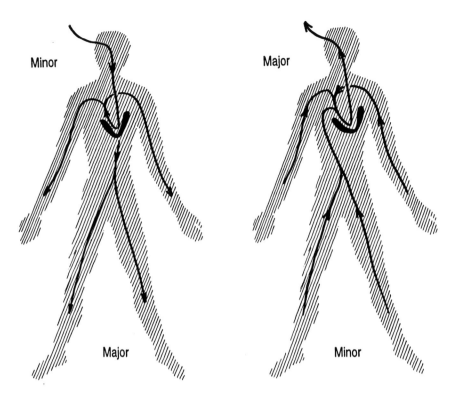

Figure 9. Left heart.   *Right heart.*

and comes to a standstill for about one tenth of a second (the so-called isometric period of cardiac cycle). Then it reverses its direction and flows centrifugally into the lungs.

The internalization which is part of inhalation intensifies to the level where the blood from the lungs flows into the left ventricle, where it accumulates back on itself once more, comes to a standstill and then flows centrifugally to the periphery of the limbs (as we mentioned above, the head is still left out of consideration at this point). In its two adjacent ventricles, the heart combines the two streams associated with the minor key — the venous blood and the arterial blood governed by inhalation — in a single diastole; with systole it transforms them into major streams. The heart transforms minor into major.

Anyone who observes the physical organization of the human being to the extent that it is dependent on the astral

body has to study physiology, not as a physicist but as a
musician. They have to understand the inner formative
power of music in the human organism (Steiner[17]).

Thus we have gained a greater awareness of our etheric and astral
bodies in sculptural and musical images. If we look back at the
modelling exercise (Figure 4, page 24) then the rhythm of expansion
and invagination appears as the image of a sculptural breathing
process of the etheric body which produces the human form. Just as
the blood flow in the mature person can be described as an after-
image of this original formative activity, respiration in the mature
person can be described as an echo of the formative activity which
flows from the etheric body when the human being develops as
embryo from out of the cosmos. Rudolf Steiner relates how in the
past, in a far-distant stage of human and earth development, human
beings in the 'Lemurian age' experienced their respiration; this was
a time when the physical part of the earth and the human organism
were much less condensed than they are today, more akin to a
steamlike state flooded with light:

The process of taking in air was still experienced by the
psyche in a soul-spiritual way as an image. It appeared in
the form of undulating tonal images which also gave shape
to the developing embryo. The soul felt itself surrounded by
surging sound and it experienced the way in which it
organized the body according to these tonal forces.[18]

This reveals the all-encompassing reality of this modelling exercise.
It leads to respiration as the motion with which the etheric and the
astral bodies musically form the physical body in rhythmical inter-
change. If we delve more deeply into the formative consequences of
this rhythm, then we see the creation of the thorax in twelve
sculptural-musical breaths (Figure 10).

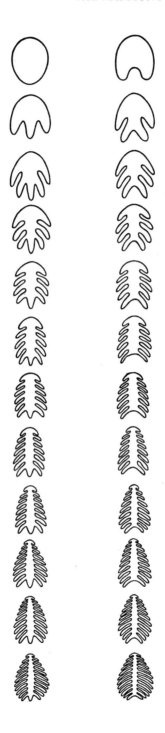

Figure 10.

5. Symptomatic illnesses:
measles and scarlet fever

These two childhood illnesses are associated with skin rashes which in their distribution allow for a symptomatic interpretation against the background of the material presented so far.

The measles rash starts at the head and spreads from there. The characteristic rash of scarlet fever generally leaves the head untouched and is concentrated in the armpits and groin. The 'measles look' is that well-known bleary appearance, since the external mucous membranes are affected: conjunctivitis, rhinitis. Other organic systems susceptible to inflammation are the lungs (pneumonia) and the larynx (laryngitis). The most serious complication is represented by the very rare acute measles encephalitis, that is, inflammation of the brain. In short, the primary areas which are affected are the respiratory system with its mucous membranes and the nervous system. Sensitivity to light is typical in the acute stages. The measles pathogen enters through the conjunctiva so that protective glasses sealed off at the sides can prevent infection.[19] In a certain sense measles are thus 'seen.' We will return to the relationship with the light ether which this implies.

As is already obvious from the distribution of the rash in scarlet fever, this disease penetrates more deeply into the inner organs. After acute angina, the heart and kidneys as well as the pancreas can suffer inflammation in rare cases — in other words, internal organs to a much greater degree. If we look in addition at the dynamics which determine the course of both illnesses, the picture is completed: measles is preceded by an early stage with a moderate rise in temperature which can appear like an uncharacteristic flu. Only with the rash does the high fever appear which, however, as a rule subsides after a few days. Scarlet fever, in contrast, is characterized by an acute start with a high fever. If, in addition, we return to the appearance of

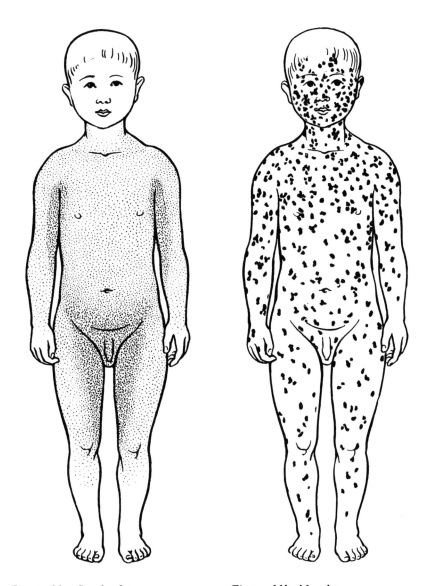

Figure 11a. Scarlet fever.   *Figure 11b. Measles.*
After Hertl, Paediatrische Differentialdiagnose

the child's face in the two cases — the weeping, bleary one of the measles child and the dry face with the clear eyes of the scarlet fever one — this overall picture accords with Rudolf Steiner's diagnosis, based on the science of the spirit. He describes how the soul and spiritual part of the child has to cope with the hereditary body. Measles occurs when the former elements prove to be too weak in relation to the physical-etheric body. As can be seen from the rash, the sculptural process which has its origins in the head has the upper hand. The physical-etheric body dominates. If the soul and spiritual element, that is the astral body and the 'I,' are strong in this struggle then scarlet fever arises and we find the inward-directed inflammations described above; the rash shows the predominance of the invaginating archetype which indicates the activity of the astral body. It is clear that the process associated with measles, which takes place to a greater extent in the physical-etheric sphere, provides the conditions in which viruses can multiply. The scarlet fever process, in contrast, which is determined to a greater degree by the astral, makes it possible for bacteria to multiply. In terms of their structure, bacteria are one step closer to animal forms than viruses. In many cases they even possess motility by means of flagella. Viruses resemble plants more closely in their construction.

In treating head-related measles, medicinal plants come into consideration which have strong root growth, such as aconite, pulsatilla or bryonia. For scarlet fever belladonna is the leading remedy. The deep-seated astral element which leads to the production of poison in this as in all the nightshades and makes this plant more animal-like, takes over the pathological process in the child. This permits the astral component in the child to withdraw from the organs and makes it easier for the child's astral constitution to re-establish its healthy relationship to the physical-etheric body.

6. Musical laws of growth

The activity of the astral body in the three-dimensional motion of the etheric body can be approached musically in a number of ways. We came to an understanding of the polarity of major and minor in the physiology of the blood and respiratory systems through a living conception of their physiological activity: through the physical direction of flow of these systems and a comparison with the inner dynamics of the musical qualities. The anatomical investigation of the way major and minor are represented in eurythmy deepened our understanding. The outer sculptural activity of the astral body still predominates completely, however, in the growing child as it develops embryologically. This activity has not yet been internalized but works in harmony with the etheric body to shape the sculptural proportions. It lives in changing relationships of size. Access to this side of astral activity is therefore found externally. The spatial relationships of size, when transferred to the monochord, reveal the musical qualities which are active in them. Since we are looking at the transformation of proportions in the progression of three-dimensional growth, time itself as the central factor in music becomes the object of investigation.

In Figure 6 those stages in the continuous growth of the child were isolated in which the relationship between the head and the body was represented by whole numbers. Thus human beings in the course of their development pass through stages in which the body is two, three, four, five, six, seven and finally eight times the size of the head. The head goes through stages in which it is one half, one third, one quarter, one fifth, one sixth, one seventh and one eighth of the overall length, with the torso and limbs correspondingly one half, two thirds, three quarters, four fifths, six seventh and seven eighths long. Such numerical relationships can be expressed musically as intervals. The interval is not simply the musical phenomenon of the life between two notes, in other words, the relationship between two notes. In terms of mathematics and physics it is also a quotient, the ratio of two numbers to be divided. If we isolate the whole-number ratios of the head to the body, we get the intervals which are accessible to our music experience. With our inner ear we can immerse ourselves in the process which takes place in the astral body during growth. Rudolf Steiner describes the way in which the astral body is active in the etheric body — in growth for example — in the following way:

> The astral body counts and differentiates, counts the etheric body. It forms it by counting. The astral body and the etheric body are linked by numbers, and numbers are something which are alive, which are active within us.[20]

Today we have largely lost an understanding of this quality of numbers, their existence as something which 'is alive, which is active in us.' But this life is still deeply familiar to musical experience. It differentiates with mathematical exactitude between 2/3 and 3/4, between a fifth and a fourth. This is the aspect of the astral which is accessible to us, and for that reason we will investigate the latter from this perspective.

In order to do this, we take a monochord and copy what the astral body does with the etheric body: we will 'count and differentiate' the relationship between the head and the body. To this end we divide the string into the ratios which reflect the relationship between the size of the head and the length of the body.[21] If we then take a violin bow we can produce a sound with the string. Let us do so first with that part of the string which becomes shorter, that is, the part corresponding to the head. If the monochord is tuned to C, the following notes are produced:

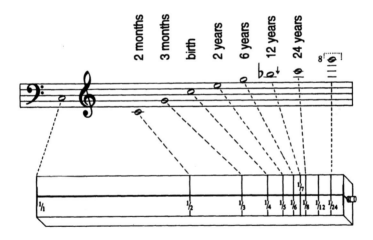

Figure 12. The monochord. The string as divided into fractions corresponding to the size of the head in relation to the body during growth (Compare Fig. 6).

What we hear, is the well-known natural harmonic series into which all processes are translated which change in a continuous ratio to one another.

So far we have worked not as musicians but as physicists. We took measurements and transposed them from the human being to a sounding string. Individual notes were created which corresponded to spatial proportions. If we further want to gain an understanding of the temporal course of development we have to grasp the relationship between the notes occurring one after the other. To this end we must listen to the quality of the intervals in the time between the spatial stages. That enables us to hear musically. Thus the transition from external, spatial relationships to the temporal developmental process forces us to take the methodological step from the physical measurement and production of sound to artistic, musical experience. In this sense the kind of listening which truly concentrates on the relationships of between notes over a period of time is of necessity a musical one. Simply registering two differently pitched notes means that one has not recognized what takes place over time between the two sounds, but one has simply compared two momentary events in the way that one does with spatial perceptions.

The range of our 'tune' comprises exactly three octaves. At this point already human nature affects the general law of 'continuous division' which in itself is unlimited: it could 'equally well' be a smaller or larger segment of the natural scale. But human beings on average grow until the head is one eighth the size of the body and then growth stops.

In music, octaves are decisive occurrences when they are experienced in the context of the diatonic scale. What happens in human beings when the octave (1/2, 1/4 and 1/8 in Figures 6 and 12) sounds? The first octave sounds between the original sphere and the first whole-number embryonic stage (Figure 6). As we saw, this octave, with which the whole melody begins, is connected with procreation through which the body emerges from the cosmic-female head. The second octave is reached with the birth of the physical body. Embryonic development reaches its conclusion at this point. This 'concluding point' is an aspect of our experience of the octave which is also relevant in the third octave. That is reached when growth stops. Under normal circumstances we do not develop a feel for what it means that human growth stops. When a purely physical and etheric being, a plant which is several years old for instance, ceases to grow, it means that it has died. Through the science of the spirit we know that the birth of the 'I,' which occurs around this time, is connected with the activity of forces of mortality.

At first glance, we therefore see three decisive events in human life connected with these three octaves: procreation (first octave), the birth of the physical body (second octave) and the birth of the 'I' (third octave). With the exactitude which is characteristic of musical experience, the octave allows us to see the dual nature of these events. On the one hand all three of them represent a conclusion, an event fulfilled. That applies particularly to procreation; for with procreation the period of human life in the spiritual world before birth, much longer in comparison to the time spent on earth, comes to an end. On the other hand the octave also contains the quality of a breakthrough into a new sphere, into a new plane of existence. The quality of a new start is based in the fact that every octave is simultaneously a new tonic.

We will understand these three octaves if we take account of the melodic intermediate steps with which they are reached. The monochord sounds may also be played on a violin — to change from a scientific to an artistic instrument.

The first octave (effective between *a* and *b* in Figure 6) is the most basic interval of all. It is the purest sound, without intermediate steps, creating the most perfect consonance which two different notes can form. The other octaves no longer sound as direct octaves but are reached through intermediate steps (see Figure 12). What becomes apparent in the step of the first octave, is the experience that human beings, whose bodies are formed under the influence of the soul quality it contains, have a fully harmonious relationship with their origins. These origins are represented in the form of the sphere.

In the octave of procreation we experience the way in which human beings make the transition from spiritual to physical forms of existence. The future 'extracephalic' physical body is still far removed from physical functions, the head has not solidified and is still as full of life as the torso and the limbs. As growth progresses, tension increasingly enters this relative equilibrium, leading to the polarity in the adult human being.

The second octave, which starts at birth, has to be heard in the following context:

Example 4.

We reach the octave through the interval of a fourth. The intervals become narrower: from the 'expanse' of the first octave we reach the 'solid' fourth via the already more inward fifth. If we want to gain a deeper understanding of the fourth, we can place it in its diatonic context:

Example 5.

The initial major second starts a flowing movement which streams through the next major second to create an inner expansiveness. Then a semi-tone follows in the sequence which constitutes the fourth, which removes us completely from the flowing, indeterminate element into a solidified, firm, closed off one. The fourth borders on the experience of meeting a barrier which denies further progress. Thus we experience musically in the fourth, which leads up to the 'birth octave,' how the embryo gradually solidifies out of the fluid element and is deposited 'on firm land' through the process of birth with its consciousness-forming force of resistance. With birth, the development of the body, in so far as it has to take place in fluid surroundings, has been concluded. Nevertheless, the way in which the fourth is 'closed off' contains an inner compulsion to continue along a new route which is different to the conclusion contained in the octave. The fourth does not allow us to come to rest in the same way that the octave does.

We therefore come to an understanding of the specific nature of an interval through the intermediate intervals which it contains. The meaning of the birth octave becomes clear through the fourth, which in turn is clarified through the semi-tone interval within it. We grasp the consciousness-waking character of birth in the fourth without its intermediate steps; we grasp the consolidating forces which underlie that in the semi-tone which it contains.

Through spiritual science we have reached an understanding of this interval which human beings in earlier times would still have had instinctively: 'For a long time human beings believed they were involved in the etheric element when they experienced the fourth. If I may put it like this, they felt the holy wind which had brought them into the physical world when they heard a fourth.'[22] The first breath taken by the human being thus represents an image which is in harmony with this characterization of the fourth.

The present standpoint will not be sufficient to understand the content of the third octave which coincides with the birth of the 'I.' This octave will be dealt with in Part Two.

Let us at this point look at a fundamental aspect of the intervals as they relate to the stages of growth. It is not the 'newborn' who corresponds to the step of a fourth. On the contrary, the fourth is present in the relationship between the stages represented in c and d in Figure 6, in other words in the temporal progression of the cephalic proportions $1/3 : 1/4 = 4/3$. We are dealing with the developmental activity of the fourth in the period between the third month and birth, and the result of that activity is then the physical proportions of the newborn (3/4 body, 1/4 head) as well as the birth process. The fourth thus deals above all with the transition from c to d which is not visible in Figure 6, as well as with the birth process. In other words, the stages in Figure 6 correspond to the notes in Figure 12. The intervals of Figure 12 provide a musical image of the forces which are formatively active in the non-visible (temporal) processes between these 'snapshots.'

This is one example of the cognitive power of art as understood by Goethe and Rudolf Steiner. The transition from spatial measurement to the observation of temporal development led us methodologically to our musical sense of hearing. The qualities of the intervals provide us with simple but concrete examples of what we called 'beauty' in the introduction. The non-material forces appear in them which create the proportions in physical development. They are musical images of the astral body, the activity of which in comparative organic development was dealt with earlier on.

At this point brief reference should be made to the relationship between the method used here, to the extent that it is based on proportions and numbers, and the work of Hans Kayser and his school. Kayser takes the step from measured proportion to musical interval. But that is where he stops. He omits to develop a living concept of the organic relationships he has investigated. He does not allow himself to relate in a musical way the relevant interval to the processes measured in space. The simple ascertainment of whole-number proportions and their intervals creates the precondition for a deeper understanding but does not provide it in itself. Kayser's research is therefore a mass of empirical material in the sculptural and musical field which needs to be developed.

We can only refer briefly here to the remaining stages. The action of the fifth leads to the stage represented in c (temporal cephalic proportions $1/2 : 1/3 = 3/2$). Qualitatively, the fifth takes an intermediate position, a kind of hypomochlion, in the equilibrium of forces between the pull to the tonic which is effective up to the fourth and the pull to the octave. The fifth is touched by the latter but not yet taken hold of. Its sound is 'no longer' given inner content by the tonic and 'not yet' by the octave. The fifth can be seen as an image for the state reached at the end of the third month of embryonic development when the organs have been formed. On the one hand human beings have emerged from the spiritual world to take on material form to the extent demonstrated by the relative conclusion of physical development, but on the other hand the inner soul life of the physical person which opens up with the octave of birth is still far removed.

Then, in the first years of life it is above all the major third (d–e C'–E') which is active; then, up to approximately age seven, it is the first larger minor third and up to the age of twelve the second smaller minor third. In this contraction of the third into the minor mood we experience the formative activity of the astral element in such a way that it gradually withdraws into itself to take on a form, a body, of its own. The third, and particularly the minor third, represents the most inwardly contracted realm in music. These forces lead to the formation of the astral body in puberty as described by the science of the spirit (birth of the astral body). That is why here, too, we see hidden the interval of a semi-tone which we already encountered as the real 'consolidating' element in the fourth at the birth of the physical body:

Example 6.

minor   major

When the semi-tone step which completes the fourth in the major key is moved backward into the province of the third, the latter turns to minor (Example 6). The major third allows the soul to expand, whereas with the minor equivalent one can feel it coming up against the barrier of the body in which it gains consciousness as a separate entity. Animals always remain in this minor mood. Their emotions are tied to the body and are satisfied through the body. Only human beings, with their self-conscious 'I,' experience emotions in their astral body, emotions which become independent of their bodily origin to the extent that they can be recalled from memory later on, that is to say without external stimuli. The activity of the 'I' in the astral body creates the human soul. It provides the facility for the emotions to expand freely as reflected in the major third. That part of the soul which is linked with the astral body is called the 'sentient soul' in anthroposophy. It can thus be observed in the major and minor third how the soul body (astral body) is expressed largely in the minor mood whereas in the major mood the (sentient) soul is 'victorious' over the soul body.[23] This explains the concurrence of the minor third with the developmental stage at which the researcher working with the science of the spirit observes the development and 'birth' of the astral body. The reason why this phase is preceded by the major third will become clear on the basis of material to be discussed below.

The notes on which we have based our observations so far (Figure 12) were produced by striking an ever-shortening string, in other words that part of the string which corresponds to the head. What notes do we produce when we do the same with the other lengthening section? While the 'head string' produces the natural harmonic series as a melodic series, the lengthening string, which corresponds to the growing torso and the limbs, produces the same natural harmonic series, but as a chordal series.[24] The same intervals now appear as chords and not as consecutive intervals. This series of chords comes about by sustaining the fundamental note which, in musical terms, acts like a pedal point (see Example 7). The peculiar effect of this type of music, which simultaneously produces the sound of head and body in its proportions, can probably only be experienced by playing it on instruments.[25]

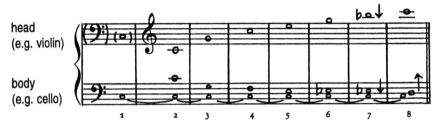

Example 7.

In general terms, the whole process is determined through the fact that what starts as harmonious octaves and fifths increasingly becomes filled with tension and intensifies. At the same time the span between the two progressions becomes steadily wider. Everything ends in an indeterminate but urgently pressing and questioning chord. It is worth noting that body and head have the procreation octave in common: the octave in chord 2 still contains tonic unison between body and head.

PART II

The Musical Physiology of Internal Organs

7. The artistic exercise in the cognition of Goethe and Haeckel

Three years before giving the modelling exercise which formed the basis of Part One, Rudolf Steiner delivered a series of lectures which were called 'Anthroposophy, its Cognitive Roots and the Fruits of its Existence.'[26] Another modelling exercise is described half-way through the course, in the fifth lecture, which we will set out here in the context of training the thinking to understand the conditions governing the existence of organisms. In preparation, Rudolf Steiner deals in the fourth lecture with the 'underlying artistry' which was at work in Goethe's and Haeckel's thinking. In the first volume of his edition of Goethe's scientific writings, Steiner already showed that the many drawings of plants which Goethe undertook were of exact methodological importance to him on his way to the concept of metamorphosis. The idea of metamorphosis in plants resides in their pattern of spatial expansion and contraction during their cycle of development.

> Since the concept is defined by a greater or lesser expansion in space as determined by the plant's generative forces, in other words, since it is to be found in that part of the plant which is immediately accessible to the eye, it is likely to be seen most easily if one begins to draw the plant in accordance with the laws of natural development. In Rome,

Goethe came across some carnations growing in a pot which demonstrated metamorphosis to him particularly clearly. In this connection he wrote: 'Seeing no means before me with which to preserve this miraculous shape, I began to draw it precisely, by which means I gained a growing insight into the basic concept of metamorphosis.' It is likely that he made more such drawings and in this way came to the concept we have been discussing.[27]

Today these drawings are accessible in *Corpus der Goethezeichnungen* and a wealth of sketches can be found there which reproduce the observations on metamorphosis he made in individual plants.

Goethe's *Italian Journey* reveals the way in which art was continuously transformed in him into an organ for the perception of the vital laws of nature.

The same is true of Haeckel, who would not have made the contribution to the natural sciences which he did if he had not investigated organisms on the basis of his natural artistic gifts, his drawing and sketching skills.[28] He drew and sketched thousands of animals at all stages of their development with a dual enthusiasm for the beauty of their colours and shapes and for the comprehensive idea which formed the basis of his perception of them. Goethe and Haeckel trained their powers of observation through their artistic activity which they practised on the objects of their study. In this way the perceptual thinking of both researchers gained more or less instinctual access to Imaginations. For C.G. Carus, too, landscape painting represented a kind of artistic research, as Meffert shows.[29]

The sculptural-musical-linguistic method attempts consciously to grasp and extend to all elements of the human constitution the tools which already assisted Goethe and Haeckel in the progress they made in organic science.

The way in which their alert scientific thinking then went on to process and represent these 'comprehensive and magnificent ideas' (Rudolf Steiner on Haeckel) was quite different in both thinkers. In each case it was related to the degree to which they were in a position consciously to observe the process of cognition within themselves. Goethe was predisposed to do this to a much greater extent than Haeckel. One need only think of the way in which he was able to respond to Schiller's assistance. Haeckel was divided between his artistic nature, which through the persistent drawing and sketching of organisms led him to the idea of evolution, and the dogmatic, indeed fanatical, evolutionary theorist in him, whose ideas were determined by and presented in materialistic ways of thinking. 'Haeckel worked with living percepts but dead concepts.'[30] Today, through the work done by Rudolf Steiner in placing Haeckel's work in the epistemological context of Goethe's methodology, we are able to separate Haeckel's achievements from the way he presented them.

The second modelling exercise, given in the lecture referred to above, is used by Rudolf Steiner to illuminate the comprehensive meaning of Haeckel's idea of the gastraea. The next step, therefore, is to set out what he meant by that.

8. Gastrulation and Haeckel's idea of the gastraea

The earliest formation of cavities in simple invertebrates occurs in gastrulation. It shows invagination as the archetypal generative expression of the astral body, as we described above. Gastrulation in various forms can also be demonstrated in vertebrates up to and including the human being.[31] On the basis of this phenomenon, Ernst Haeckel developed the idea of the archetypal animal, which he called 'gastraea.' He thought that every animal had descended from the gastraea through heredity and adaption.[32] The embryonic development of coral, (Figure 13), is taken from his *Anthropogenie*. The first stage is the blastocyst which is filled with fluid. The process of invagination is described by Haeckel in a way which makes the plasticity of the perceptive power of his thinking clearly evident in his words:

Now a very important and noteworthy process begins,
namely the invagination of the blastocyst. The sphere with
its single layer of cells becomes a cup with a double layer
of cells. At a given point the surface of the sphere begins to

flatten and deepen into a hollow. This hollow becomes
deeper and deeper. It expands at the expense of the inner
blastocoel or cleavage cavity. The latter decreases to the
extent that the former increases. Finally the inner blastocoel
disappears altogether as the invaginated part of the
blastoderm (or the wall of the cavity) meets the outer non-
invaginated part of the same. At the same time the cells of
both parts take on a different shape and size. The inner cells
become more rounded, whereas the outer ones begin to
lengthen. Thus the embryo takes on the form of a cup or
juglike body, the wall of which consists of two layers of
cells and whose inner cavity is open to the outside at one
end (the original place of invagination). We describe this
most important and interesting embryonic form as gastrula.[33]

On the basis of the 'basic law of biogenesis,' according to which
every organism recapitulates in its embryonic development the overall
evolution of its ancestors, Haeckel uses the gastraea to develop the
following thought:

The human being and all other animals which at the
beginning of their individual development pass through a
twin layer phase or a gastrula form, must have originated
from an ancient simple root form whose body throughout its
life consisted only of two different layers of cells or germ
layers (as still happens with the lowest plantlike animals).
Let us give this ancient root form the name gastraea (that is,
primitive intestine animal).[34]

The idea of the gastraea is a hypothetical construction of Haeckel's.
He wanted to use it to establish the monophyletic origin of all
animals. In this form his idea has (rightly) been relegated to obscurity
by science. Looked at from a Goethean perspective, however, the
gastraea represents the three-dimensional image of the spiritual animal
archetype which in its physical expression causes the histological
differentiation between endoderm and ectoderm. The gastraea, as the
archetypal animal in Goethe's sense, falls into the same category as
the archetypal plant. Both have in common the developmental pattern
of extension and contraction, or expansion and invagination.[35]

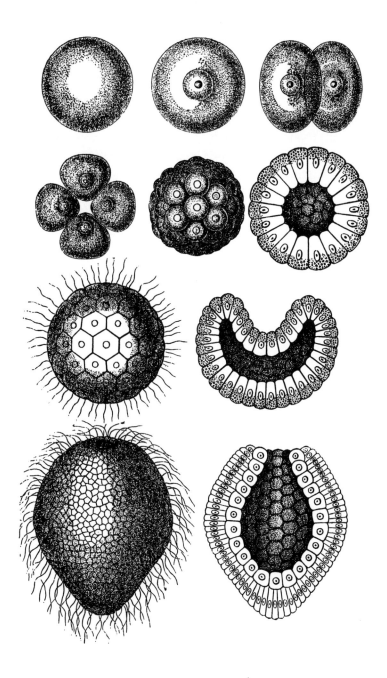

Figure 13. Gastrulation of a coral. From E. Haeckel, Anthropogenie, *p.I.158.*

9. The inversion exercise

In Haeckel an idea emerged with the 'gastraea,' whose power as a means of understanding the world of organisms was salvaged by Rudolf Steiner. Haeckel had deprived it of any usefulness by thinking of it in physical terms and placing it at the beginning of a hereditary mechanism which was to form the basis for the animal kingdom. Rudolf Steiner understood the gastraea as what it really was: an idea. And he placed it in its context within the world of ideas. He subsequently dedicated to Ernst Haeckel one of the books in which he moved the gastraea idea into the right light.[36] A process thus took place between Haeckel and Rudolf Steiner which is similar to the one between Goethe and Schiller, when the latter made Goethe aware that the archetypal plant was not something that could be experienced by the senses, but was an idea. The difference was that Haeckel was unable to make anything of Rudolf Steiner's clarification.

When you open Haeckel's writings and look·at the drawings which he made of the initial stages of embryonic life, stages in which he wanted to show how the ontogenesis of a being represents an abbreviated phylogenic development, you will

Figure 14. Rudolf Steiner's inversion exercise (Drawing: Daniel Moreau).

find drawings which, if you knew what they looked like, would remind you of the instinctive Imaginations of the ancient initiates. Others made such drawings as well, but for him they became the cornerstone of his thinking. Haeckel studied gastrulation, the initial stage of embryonic development in which the cup shape is formed and during which the cells develop in a way similar to the invagination of a sphere. And in his imagination he constructed the gastraea, a hypothetical organism which once had such a form in phylogenetic development, a form which is repeated in this early stage of embryonic development, in gastrulation. (Steiner[37]).

Rudolf Steiner makes this easier to understand by illustrating it with a series of sculptural forms which formed the basis for specific exercises in certain esoteric schools which he does not specify. Such exercises were intended to stimulate the Imaginative perception of a process which at first sight appears to have no connection whatsoever with Haeckel's line of thinking. They teach one to understand how cognition is formed out of the human bodily components. We will return to this initially puzzling link between embryonic and cognitive development later, but first the exercise itself:

Imagine that you have an elastic sphere. You make an indentation in the top in such a way that what was pointing

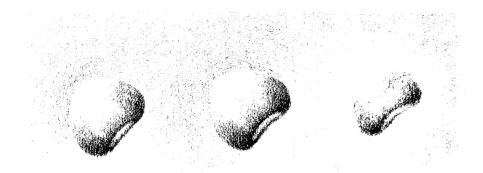

upwards has now been pressed to face downwards so that
the sphere turns into a kind of bowl or plate. Imagine
further that the sphere is folded in on itself not only until
the indentation touches the lower wall at the bottom, but
passes beyond it, penetrating it as it were. But as it comes
out the other side, its substance has changed consistency so
that the sphere, having been penetrated in this way, appears
to be surrounded by light — but light which has been
produced by its own invaginated part. This is a figure which
cannot be drawn that easily, but which exemplifies in a
simple way what was to be represented in such esoteric
societies symbolically as the cognitive process, in order to
stimulate an understanding of the latter in those who were
meant to learn by it (Steiner[38]).

While in the 'limb exercise,' as we will call the sculptural exercise of
1924 from now on, the centre of the sphere remaines untouched, the
process here involves the penetration of the centre (compare Figure
14).

This infolding too is caused by the central physical forces in which
the paralysing, devitalizing influence of the astral body can embody
itself. When the process of invagination reaches the core, it has
reached the centre of its own vitality and from this point it acquires
a new quality. It begins to move centrifugally towards the outside.
Thus the infolded internal space enlarges in the same direction as the
expansion of the limb exercise. This means that we now have to refer
to it as an inner expansion. When it reaches the opposite wall of the
sphere a new quality occurs once again: the invagination process has
passed through the whole of the interior space of the sphere and is
now divided from external space only through a single point. The
interior and exterior surface are combined in this point. If this 'skin'
is penetrated the power whose motion has been transformed from an
infolding, centripetal one into inner expansion combines freely with
the etheric forces flowing in from the cosmos. Inversion has taken
place from physical, gravitational space into the etheric counter-space
of light.

This exercise develops beyond external, three-dimensional space. In
order to understand what is happening we have to utilize concepts like

those of geometry, for instance. The inner life of the whole process is only disclosed to the musical ear. Our understanding from a purely sculptural perspective ends at the point where the astral body suppresses the life forces to the extent that it can come to expression. Only the musical ear can follow these processes which move beyond three-dimensional space into the soul arena.

Conversely, the content of such an Imaginative exercise can be acquired through the forms of the physical organs in so far as they have been determined by the Imaginative generative action of the etheric body. For 'it is through the physical that we see the etheric form; but it is the etheric form which we really see and the physical form is only the means by which we can see the etheric' (Steiner[39]). Our sculptural and musical method seeks to grasp in living concepts the mobile, fluid life of the world of etheric images, whose accuracy cannot be established from within itself; it does so anatomically on the basis of the physical body and musically on the basis of the astral body. Thus we will apply the inversion exercise anatomically, then return to Haeckel and finally attempt to penetrate it musically.

The formation of thoughts, which this exercise is designed to illuminate, takes place in the head. That is why we will examine the extent to which the phenomenon of inversion is present anatomically and physiologically in the transition from the torso to the head.

10. The anatomy of inversion

10.1 In the skeleton

In the skull, the skeleton is the outer covering, the 'organ-capsule.' In the rest of the body it provides the inner framework. The brain thus resides in an inverted skeleton. We will examine more closely below how and when this inversion takes place. Even from a skeletal perspective the formation of thoughts thus already resides in an inverted space in relation to the rest of the skeleton.

10.2 In the sensory system

The development of the eye illustrates the inversion process in the head zone in a particularly typical fashion. At first the brain vesicle undergoes invagination in the same way that we have already seen happening in the neural tube. The process passes through the centre of the vesicle and touches the other side of the 'cup.' As if in answer to this contact, the infolded tissue begins a further differentiation process to transform itself into the retina. This inner invaginative action is answered by a similar movement from the outside, in which a piece of skin (ectoderm) is brought to the inside, which then forms the lens. At the point where the lens becomes transparent the whole process has reached the stage of inversion: what began as a separate movement inwards in the form of the eye vesicle has broken through to the light on the opposite side.

Figure 15. The development of the eye in vertebrates (from Duke Elder, p.30)

10.3 In the nervous system

What we have come to know as sculptural metamorphoses become visible on an organic level in the anatomy of the nervous system. The initial sphere which forms the large head in the embryo corresponds from an organic perspective to the rapidly developing brain. The expansion of nervous substance into the torso and the limbs is mirrored on the level of fine tissue in the construction of the nerve cells. What distinguishes nerve tissue from other sorts of body tissue is that the cell nucleus and the cell body are often far apart. The so-called nerve fibre is in fact the very much expanded and lengthened cell body of the nerve cell. Thus the cell body of a nerve cell whose nucleus is positioned in a ganglion of the spinal cord in the region of the loins can extend as far as the toes.

Thus two polar areas of tissue are created in the nervous system. On the one hand there is the zone comprising the nuclei which is essentially centred on the spinal cord and the brain. This collection of cell nuclei from the nerve cells is described by its appearance as 'grey matter.' On the other hand there are the fibre areas, which in their capacity as pathways form the link between the periphery of sensory and muscular activity and the centres of the spinal cord and brain. Because of their colour they are called 'white matter.' The areas of the nuclei ('grey matter') are arranged centrally in the spinal cord, coated by the mass of fibres, the 'white matter.' If we follow the continuation into the cerebrum this arrangement changes completely. In the cerebrum the grey matter lies on the periphery as the co-called 'cerebral cortex.' It surrounds the white matter which lies within it.

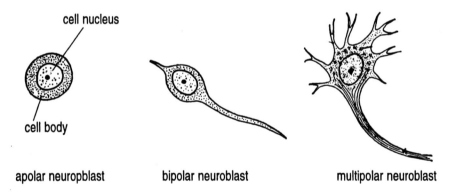

cell nucleus

cell body

apolar neuropblast   bipolar neuroblast   multipolar neuroblast

Figure 16. The development of the nerve cells (from Langman).

With the transition from the spinal cord to the inverted skeletal space of the skull, the network of nerves also changes its spatial orientation. The right side crosses over to the left and pathways which up to that point run on the left cross over to the right (which is the reason why the right side of the body is connected with the left cerebral hemisphere and vice versa). Pathways which lie at the front move to the back and those at the back to the front. The area where this transition takes place is called the 'brain stem.'

> In the transition from the spinal cord to the brain there is a complete structural transformation which takes place in a brief transitional zone ... The more or less uniform arrangement of grey and white matter which a cross-section of the spinal cord shows at all levels, is transformed fundamentally in the brain stem and changes from one cross-section to the next. Grey matter no longer appears in the self-contained form of the centrally positioned H-shape but is spread over the whole of the cross-section in single nerve cells or in groups of them. The fibres of white matter mostly run diagonally crossways (Elze[40]).

The nervous system thus undergoes an inversion process on the way from the spinal cord to the brain. What we see as a finished result in the skeleton is active in the nervous system as a functional process to the extent that every impulse from the periphery to the brain, or in reverse, has to go through such an inversion. Furthermore, the nervous system displays the same morphological polarity as is evident in the skeleton in the round bones of the limbs and the flat surfaces of the skull bones:

> The fibres in the cerebrum display a very characteristic shape. While they are combined in round threads and bundles in the rest of the central nervous system with the exception of the cerebellum, they are arranged in thin, narrow plates in the cerebrum (Elze[41]).

Not all parts of the brain, however, are affected by the inversion process. Numerous sections of nuclei within the areas which are part of the 'old' brain (diencephalon, mesencephalon) are surrounded here, too, by their pathways like in the spinal cord. Essentially it is the cerebrum which is inverted as far as grey and white matter is concerned, forming that part of the brain which, in the way that it overlies the old parts of the brain, has developed most strongly in human beings, in contrast to the animals. This has now provided us with a functional perspective: it is through the inverted cerebrum — in connection of course with all the other human characteristics of the organism — that we possess alert, self-conscious thinking. The older

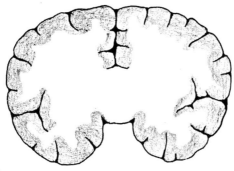

Figure 17.
Frontal section
through the cerebrum.

Figure 18.
Transverse section
through the spinal chord.

non-inverted parts of the brain are not able to make the vital processes of the organs which they control fully conscious. That is why they appear only on a feeling and will level as instinctual impulses.

10.4 In the muscular system

The muscular system is also affected by such inversion in the region of the neck. 'The muscular surfaces at the hyoid bone give a clear picture of the high degree of confusion between body and head muscles in this area ...' (By seeing which muscles belong to the head and which to the body) 'the apparent chaos in the innervation of these muscles becomes comprehensible' (Braus[42]). In the same way that we have to refer to 'scattered groups of nerve cells' in the inversion zone of the nervous system, here too we find the dissolution of the order which applies in the 'extra-cephalic human being' (Rudolf Steiner). This phenomenon of chaos in the inversion zone will concern us further later on in the treatment of these processes from a musical point of view. But it also corresponds to the sculptural exercise, since the floor of the cup is destroyed when inversion begins.

10.5 In the blood system

The inversion of the vascular system and the blood itself occurs in the network of blood vessels in the ventricles of the brain. Their embryonic development is self-explanatory in view of what has gone before: the brain begins the infolding process and takes the blood vessels with it. Once inside, the network of vessels developing there ('choroid plexus') begins to produce the cerebrospinal fluid. First of all it fills the inner ventricles of the brain and flows downwards from there to the level of the foramen magnum, the large hole in the occipital bone at the base of the head. Here, in the inversion region there are three small openings through which the cerebrospinal fluid exits to circulate round the outside of the brain. The inner has turned into the outer cerebrospinal fluid which gives buoyancy to the brain. These three openings (the foramina of Luschkae and Magendi) are the anatomical correlation of the rim which is produced as the sphere is inverted.

The exit holes of the cerebrospinal fluid are indeed created embryonically through a tear in the previously slightly curved wall of the neural tube (Starck[43]).

The blood supplies the metabolism of the brain and thereby gives sustenance to its physical nature. The cerebrospinal fluid relieves the brain of its weight by giving it buoyancy according to the principle of Archimedes. The same power of the etheric body which through the muscles allows the physical body to counter the force of gravity is active in the fluid of the brain, enabling waking consciousness and the participation of the breathing in our thinking life (Husemann[44]).

Thus we encounter inversion here in the following way:

> the blood becomes cerebrospinal fluid
> heaviness becomes buoyancy

We will deal with the exact physiology of the cerebrospinal fluid in our musical investigation of inversion.

Finally, the quality of inversion in the head is shown in the way that respiration affects the paranasal sinuses, which take in air with exhalation and release air with inhalation. The principle of inversion

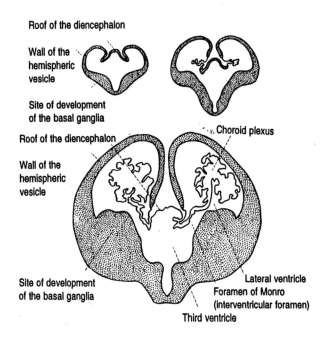

Roof of the diencephalon

Wall of the hemispheric vesicle

Site of development of the basal ganglia

Choroid plexus

Roof of the diencephalon

Wall of the hemispheric vesicle

Site of development of the basal ganglia

Lateral ventricle

Foramen of Monro (interventricular foramen)

Third ventricle

Figure 19. The embryological development of the brain ventricles and their vascular network (choroid plexus). (From H. Brans, Lehrbuch, *Vol.III, p.396.)*

in the head also makes it possible to understand why, from the perspective of the limb exercise, the direction of flow of arterial and venous blood is reversed in the vessels supplying the brain (see page 30).

This generic unitary principle of inversion allows us to understand the creative action of the etheric body on a non-material level at the point where the organism no longer applies its generative forces to the physical body, but transforms them into the conceptual and imaginative life of the mind. Through self-observation we can see that in this respect the etheric body comes under the influence of the ego-organization. Physical organic tissue is extended by the etheric body, invaginated by the astral body and inverted by the ego-organization.

If we compare this exercise with the one which was given three years later, we notice that the latter exercise for the outer form of the human being leads to the limb structure. The former exercise penetrates inward and provides insight into the way that feeling arises

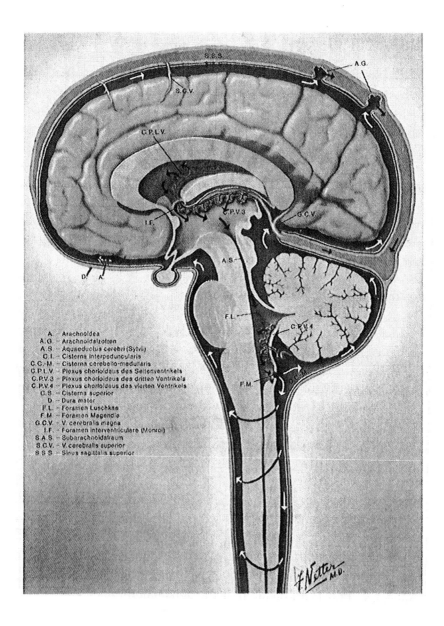

Figure 20. Sagittal section through the brain and spinal chord. Black arrows denote inner, white arrows denote outer cerebrospinal fluid.

in animals and cognition in human beings. Thus the limb exercise
leads to an understanding of the etheric body in its outer quality as
will. The inversion exercise leads to the inner transformation of the
generative forces into the power of thinking. (Although Rudolf Steiner
speaks of an 'elastic sphere,' it is evident from the limb exercise
which was explained in Part One that the exercise is also meant to be
taken in a sculptural sense. It goes on to refer to gastrulation as
sculptural invagination in the organism.[45])

10.6 In the utterance of words

The transition to language was already touched upon in connection
with the physiology of exhaling (see page 29). The blood in the veins
carries in it the dissolved and decayed matter which human beings
continually produce. As we exhale, we excrete this poison. Almost at
the point of excretion, the muscles of the larynx are able to stem the
outflowing air and transform it into sound. The sound is formed into
utterances through the organs located above the larynx in the head.
Through the 'I,' new spiritual life is infused into the dead end-product
of the metabolic process, thus forming language. This inversion of the
metabolic products of the physical body into the life of the spirit takes
place in the same region where, further back, inversion takes place in
the skeletal structure, the blood and the nervous systems.

> The human larynx is nothing more than an atrophied human
> head, a head which cannot quite become that, and therefore
> gives expression to its headlike qualities in human language.
> Human language is the persistent attempt, in the medium of
> air, of the larynx to become head.[46]

Language contains the essence of the activity of the 'I' to the extent
that the latter fills the sound made by the astral body, also produced
by animals, with meaning. The physiological and anatomical content
of the inversion exercise is illustrated in the inversion of the head and
of the word. The exercise demonstrates how cognition as it develops
in language and in the thinking is based on this inversion process. The
deceased body takes on a form which begins to resound and is
illuminated by the light of consciousness. This transformation of the

body is represented in the image of the serpent consuming its tail. The consumption of the living form in the inversion process releases the spiritual illumination which was tied down in the organs. Rudolf Steiner describes this Imagination as the essence of the sculptural inversion exercise:

> One symbol coming up again and again was used to depict the Imaginative perception of the process of cognition in man himself. The process was not described in a way that an epistemologist would do so. It was beheld in a form of instinctive clairvoyance, and they represented what they saw by drawing a picture of a serpent biting its own tail. That image showed a major characteristic of the process of attaining knowledge. But in fact the picture I have described to you is only something that came to be used later, more or less for popular presentation. The actual symbolic images were carefully guarded secrets in the groups, guarded because there was a certain desire for power, the desire to be the ones in the know while others were not in the know. The picture shown in public, of the serpent biting its own tail, should in fact be the image of a serpent that not merely bites its own tail but swallows it, as it were. As much of the tail as enters into the mouth becomes spiritualized. And then something would show itself that would need to be painted in subtler colours — if the serpent itself had been painted in strong colours — as a kind of aura for the serpent. The result was a somewhat more complex image. If we try to express it in simple words, we need to use the expression Dr Unger was using in his lecture this morning, though he actually kept apologizing for using it. (It is indeed necessary, in a way, to apologize for many things, even if they are perfectly justifiable today, when speaking on the basis of anthroposophy.) Dr Unger repeatedly used the term 'invert.'

There follows a description of the inversion exercise which we have already encountered. Rudolf Steiner was at pains to place Haeckel's gastraea in the context of this exercise. On a natural scientific basis, Haeckel develops an archetypal animal form which he only thinks of in physical and material terms. In reality, this form is one stage in the

Figure 21. Title vignette of the drama The Souls' Awakening *by Rudolf Steiner.*

Imaginative sequence of images with which the transformation of matter through the astral body (invagination) and the 'I' (inversion) was perceived in ancient times.

Haeckel the natural scientist had discovered an Imagination without being aware of it. The path which seeks the spirit in nature had crossed the path which leads to the spirit inwardly in one's own soul.

> I am mentioning something to you that may be of no interest whatsoever to many people today, yet it must be regarded by anyone following the path of knowledge with integrity, as a truly outstanding fact in cultural development. Haeckel drew the outside world and arrived at the beginnings of symbolic figures that were considered highly esoteric in an earlier age, figures still preserved here and there, though very much in secret. Within certain power-hungry organizations it is considered downright treason to speak of them. In the past, these figures had emerged from an inner experience; they were records of instinctive Imaginations. This means nothing less but that science has arrived at a point — in progressing to insight into processes within the animal organism — where scientists have to draw things representing external processes in the same way as long ago people drew what emerged from an imaginative life that arose freely in the soul, achieving cosmic insight by intesification of the inner life. Inner experience was used to create symbols that completely and utterly resemble those now achieved by drawing what is seen in the outside world. More and quite different ones will be found as science

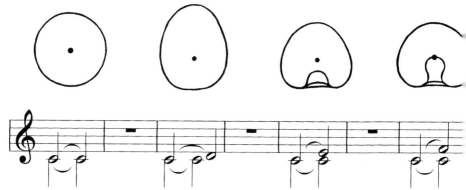

Figure 22. The musical structure of the inversion exercise (see text)
Example 8.

progresses. This is an utterly outstanding fact in the history
of cultural development.[47]

Why was it, then, that the early stages of embryonic development
led Haeckel to discover the archetypal form which, when pursued into
the Imaginative sphere, leads to an understanding of the process of
cognition? This step contains the secret of the transformation of the
generative forces from their reproductive function into the activity
connected with the formation of concepts, as investigated by Rudolf
Steiner.[48]

In order to gain an insight into this 'ensoulment' and spiritualiza-
tion of the generative forces we have to begin by coming to grips with
the musical structure of the inversion exercise.

11. The musical structure of
the inversion exercise

When the inversion process takes place in the human being's etheric
body through the activity of the 'I' in the astral body, the question
arises, from a musical perspective, whether there are phenomena
which reflect this process musically. Is there a sequence in the musical
motion of the astral body in the middle of which a new quality takes

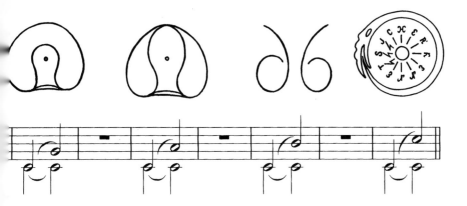

over and at the end of which our feeling breaks through to a different plane? In this context we can look at the diatonic scale, which is particularly accessible to our present consciousness, in the major key for instance (Figure 22 and Example 8).

The self-contained wholeness of the sphere, which combines within itself both the earliest embryonic stage and the highest level of completion, can be found musically in the experience of the prime: the restfulness of unison with itself. The hidden nature of the prime is only revealed in the light of the octave, which in turn contains a new prime in embryonic form. The next stage, the duality of the egg-shaped form, introduces a movement into the quiet of the sphere which does not, however, yet contain anything of an inward nature. Life, the original motion, begins with the second. All further steps are seconds with a changing soul content. The original second itself does not yet contain anything of an inner nature. It is an external, purely sculptural life; we can admire it with amazement in sparkling runs and trills — with 'amazement' because we cannot immerse ourselves inwardly in the rapid flow of the second. The start of Beethoven's Piano Sonata Op. 27 No. 1 (see Example 33, page 215) provides a nice example of the contrast between the inner life of the third and the outer life of the second.

In form three, sculptural existence turns inward in the same way as the third opens up to make room for our feeling life. Sphere, egg shape and invagination can be seen as the three-dimensional expression of the intervals. With step four the feeling life takes hold of its own centre; the forces of invagination take hold of themselves. This step can be clearly experienced in the fourth. It is like waking from the dreamlike state of the third to find oneself in the centre of one's being, in the 'I.'

As we come to shape five, we have to think of the intervals in the context of the whole scale. Up to the fourth we experience a strong relationship to the prime. This is due to the fact that up to this point the centre of the sphere has been preserved. But from the fifth onward the qualities of the intervals begin to develop their own inner flow; the octave begins to exert a mysterious influence although it has not yet sounded. The sixth is filled with its light and the seventh fuses with it. Thus we experience this inner expansion as the first stage at which the physical centre of the form has disappeared: the fifth, detached from its root but still lacking resolution. In form six the inner and the outer surface have fused into a single point. Inner and outer are united in a single point in space. Musically one experiences the sixth as filled with the light of the octave without, however, losing one's sense of self. One is not yet sucked into the light as happens in the seventh. With the latter the floor of the cup is torn open and the world of the octave appears.[49]

What shape, then, is formed by the octave? On reaching the octave, the substance which has been transformed into light is undoubtedly given a new form and brought to rest. The octave unveils the secret which is hidden in the prime. A new sphere is formed in the octave from the light of inversion.

In this way the seven elements of the astral body manifest themselves on a sculptural and Imaginative level, making room for the seven intervals to unfold as action of the will. Its first element, with which it inhabits the physical laws, is the prime; the second is the etheric element; the third is the element with which it lives in itself (the major variant corresponding more to the sentient soul, the minor variant more to the astral body). In the fourth we hear the life of the intellectual soul in the astral body; in the fifth the astral body touches the spirit of the octave with the consciousness soul, taking hold of the former in the sixth. Thus we can experience today in the major sixth the future element of the spirit self. The life spirit in the astral body is grasped through the seventh and the spirit man in the octave. These were the conclusions reached by Walter Blume on the basis of Rudolf Steiner's notes. Steiner commented on his work:

The application of the findings of the science of the spirit to music in this way cannot be faulted. Nevertheless, care should be taken in applying this kind of observation to other arts in exactly the same way. It is possible with music precisely because the inner proportions of the 'I' are exactly mirrored as unconscious proportions in the astral sphere.[50]

12. Generation and flow of the cerebrospinal fluid

We seek to introduce certainty into the relationship between the uncertain world of etheric images and reality from two perspectives. From the perspective of the physical body on the one hand and from the musical structure of the tonal world in the astral body on the other hand. For this reason we will use the series of sculptural and musical images once again to look at the embryological and functional anatomy of the cerebrospinal fluid system (compare page 64f).

At the start of brain development, at the stage of the brain vesicle, this is equivalent to the sphere and its extension. The invagination of the third phase guides the branching blood vessels to the inside. The fourth step, taking hold of the centre, takes place physiologically in the thickening of the blood vessels to form the vascular membranes at the centre of the brain. The etheric body is tied to the physical body in the blood through protein and the heavy metal iron. The vascular membranes (choroid plexuses) thicken in the centre of the brain through the process connected with the fourth. The blood, which has flowed to this point from outside into the cavity caused by invagination, now secretes the cerebrospinal fluid in the fifth stage. In the step to the fifth blood turns to watery fluid. The cells, iron, protein, fibrin — in short, the physical elements which bind the etheric body to the

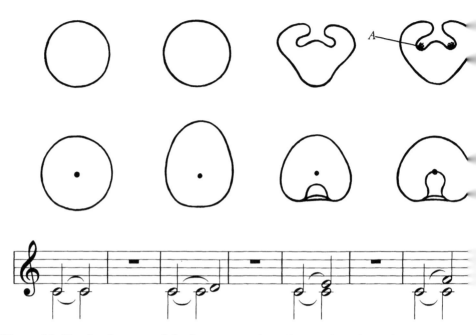

Figure 23. The development of the brain ventricles (phase 1-4) and the flow of the cerebrospinal fluid (phase 5-7). (See text.) Not included in the diagram are the blood vessels growing inwards from above which thicken into the choroid plexuses (A). Stage two is not visible here since the lengthwise growth of the brain takes place downwards at right angles to the plane of projection. The diagram as a whole illustrates inversion in the physical, etheric and astral body.

physical body — are prevented from continuing their flow into the brain ventricles. We experience this musically in the fifth as the severance from the forces of the prime. We can see in the choroid plexuses how in the step from fourth to fifth on a sculptural and musical level those parts of the fluid human being are excluded from the blood which bind the etheric body to the formation and preservation of the physical body. Here once again we have the activity of the thinking, as described in *The Philosophy of Freedom,* which is preparing its ground. It pushes back the physical organization and takes its place. The activity of the thinking, in preparing to manifest itself, is the same as the activity of the etheric body — first forming the physical body in which its thought processes are then reflected.[51]

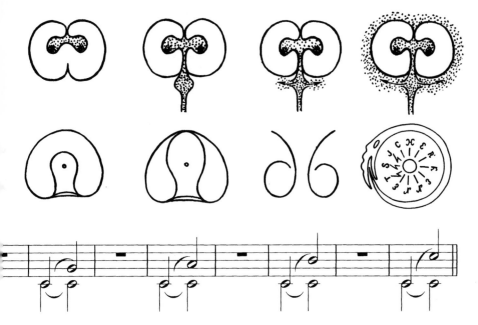

The etheric body which flows in the blood is suddenly deprived, with the transformation of blood into watery fluid, of the tools with which it forms the physical body. It loses its hold in the pure, slightly salty fluid; but it is taken hold of by the astral body which agitates this fluid through respiration. The generative activity of the etheric body, liberated from the physical body, becomes conscious in the astral body through respiration. Life forces turn into 'experience.' Every artistic, every thought experience arises because respiration intercepts in the cerebrospinal fluid the motions of the etheric body which are set off in the latter through sensory perception or through the development of ideas.

In step six this internal fluid circulates to the outer limits of the ventricles of the brain through the so-called cerebral aqueduct. In the inversion region of the cerebellum it reaches these limits and in the seventh stage flows out through the three small openings.

Following inversion, the centre is taken hold of through the formation of the choroid plexuses. Then the internal expansion forces seek to leave the inner ventricles in the form of the cerebrospinal fluid. Having exited in the step connected with the seventh, it flows round the brain as outer cerebrospinal fluid in the process associated with the octave, providing buoyancy for the brain.

The sixth sculptural stage, in which the opposite wall becomes thin, but does not break, remains in certain animals. Here the fluid exits by means of diffusion. 'Often these regions form a bubble like evagination ... whose epithelium becomes very thin and tears at the embryonic stage in most mammals.'[52]

Through this inversion, then, the etheric body is separated from the physical body in the fluid human being. Instead, it unites with the astral body which penetrates the cerebrospinal fluid through respiration. This process reveals qualities of the head which were fixed in the preceding stages of embryonic development, namely that the etheric body resonates in harmony with the astral body in the cerebrospinal fluid. The generative forces are thus enabled to enter the consciousness as living forces. In the metabolism and the limbs the etheric forces are concerned with the revitalization and preservation of the physical body. The astral body works to dissolve form in this sphere. In the head the etheric body is forced out of the physical body and is brought into harmony with the respiratory rhythm of the astral body. By this means the activity of the etheric body is brought to consciousness in the head. The astral body, combined with this part of the etheric body, was described by Rudolf Steiner, with reference to the cosmic period of the old moon, as 'a wonderful musical instrument on which cosmic harmonies can be made to sound.'[53] In that period this process allowed the forces to enter which sculpted the body musically, forces which today we experience inwardly through inversion as being connected with the consciousness. In other words, we experience inwardly in the period of earth development what at the start of the book we characterized as the sculptural stream which flows from the head into the limbs. This sculptural stream, which is imbued with the harmony of the spheres, with 'Abel music,' predominates in that stage of embryonic development which is the recapitulation on earth of the old moon period. We can begin to get an inkling of the way in which human beings in the future, through their experience of the sixth, the seventh and the octave, will develop a conscious understanding of the harmonies of the spheres sounding in the body.

The type of thinking which is tied to the senses, which understands the laws of mechanics and of physical matter is linked to the inner extension of the senses, the brain. The living thinking which is at home in the archetype and its metamorphosis into different forms is brought to consciousness in the cerebrospinal fluid. Thus Rudolf Steiner speaks several times specifically about the 'fluid nature' of the archetype.[54] It is the awakening of our own embryonic generative forces in the consciousness.

Example 9. Beethoven Op. 28, conclusion of the final movement.

It is difficult to imagine such a process from reading a book. For that we require the musical experience on which the material presented here is based. In every final movement, the overall form of a classical piece comprising several movements takes on the characteristic of the seventh. Not only in the sense that the development of the last movement is driven harmonically towards the end of the piece by the dominant seventh chord, but it lies in the overall nature of classical final movements to be subject to this kind of momentum. The following example is the closing coda of the final movement of Beethoven's Sonata in D major, Op. 28. If it is true that in musical terms inversion corresponds to the action of the seventh and the octave, then we are able to experience in the closing bars of this finale the dammed up and breaking waves of the liberated etheric.

Since the real manifestation of the octave, which is the goal of this process, is still closed off to present-day consciousness, the final cad-

Figure 24. Cast of the ventricles containing cerebrospinal fluid seen from the side (left = front). (Drawing, from a model, by Daniel Moreau.)

ence ends in two slim chords of an almost provisional nature which are so porous that they do not absorb the momentum which has been created but allow it to pass through them into inaudible realms.

Thus we can begin to understand in musical terms the physiology of the head as revealed to the Imaginative consciousness:

> ... something very notable happens in the head of human beings. Because everything of a soul and spiritual nature is dammed up there, it foams back like water when it reaches a weir. In other words, the matter carried by the soul and spirit, like the Mississippi carries silt, foams back inwardly in the brain so.that cross-currents can be found in the brain where the soul and spiritual element is dammed up. (Steiner[55]).

Now we are inwardly prepared to experience the three-dimensional forms which exist invisibly in the brain as fluid-containing cavities. If we make a cast of the brain ventricles and remove the surrounding brain substance, we create in positive form the three-dimensional image of the negative counter-space which our etheric body uses to liberate itself through inversion.

13. Reproduction and thinking

We must now answer the following question: How are we to interpret Haeckel's construction of the animal archetype from his observation of embryonic development, if, at the same time, that way of thinking turns out to be a stage in an Imaginative series of forms which illustrate the transformation of physical generative forces into the power of thinking?

Let us recall our earlier ideas about the process of fertilization.

The mother exposes the germ cell to the expansive influence of the environment through the fact that she is constitutionally more deeply immersed in the sculptural stream. The female ovum expands to become the largest of all the body cells. The male sperm cell is compressed by the physical and mineral forces. Thus the mother conceives the spiritual embryo of the individual, who has already descended to the level of the etheric world in the form of the original, Imaginatively perceived head sphere — a form which still contains all the elements which will be released through fertilization. From the father, the embryo receives the capacity, as we saw, to extend the sphere to form the 'extra cerebral' elements — torso and limbs (see page 27).

What happens when we try to understand a physical occurrence? We combine external perception with concepts from within ourselves. It is simply a matter of the intensity with which we conduct our thinking as to whether we observe the ideas which serve to put our perceptions into context as living ideas. This becomes evident in truly active and not machine-like passive thinking. The world of ideas from which we take the concept we combine with sensory perception is, as we noted in the introductory chapters, the etheric world. Which is why Rudolf Steiner describes the etheric world as flooded with cosmic thoughts.

In the process of acquiring knowledge, we receive — or better, take hold of — the idea in its concrete cosmic existence and combine it with sensory perception. We therefore become 'maternal' in every productive act of knowledge, that is, one which we have truly arrived at ourselves, in so far we receive the living idea from the etheric world and take the sensory perception as the physical-paternal element. Both combine to provide the fruits of knowledge. And fruitful knowledge which is produced in this living and active way continues to develop during the course of one's life, even if one is not always aware of it.

> Just as two principles are united in the physical act of fertilization, the male and the female, so they unite in the product of the creative person. The artist, the philosopher often take their material from outside and add to it from within themselves the artistic, the philosophical form. In saying this, I am not merely speaking metaphorically, but am referring to something for which natural phenomena provide good evidence (Steiner[56]).

But how did the capacity to think arise in human development in the first place? According to research carried out by the science of the spirit, androgynous human beings existed in the very far distant past.

We already referred to this ancestor of ours, who with his own breath formed his body, on page 37. At that time the fertilization of the germ cell consisted of the soul-spirit touching the latter. In this way the germ cell developed in accordance with the commencing respiratory movement of the soul. Now, the human soul is male and female at the same time in so far as feeling is polarized into forces of the will and the imagination.

> [For] the soul is male and female at the same time. It contains both aspects. Its male element is related to what is described as the will, its female element to the imagination. The physical evolution of the earth has resulted in the body assuming a one-sided form. The male body has taken on a form which is determined by the will, whereas the female one shows all the characteristics of imagination (Rudolf Steiner[57]).

We have no difficulty in understanding that because we have already grasped the female characteristics in the way that ideas are conceived. In the course of the steadily increasing density of the earth, it gradually became impossible for human beings to bring all the forces active in their development to physical incarnation. Their bodies could absorb only a part of the generative and soul forces, either the female of the male part. That part of the creative and soul forces which was not able to assume a physical incarnation thus became available for purely inner soul activity, for the formation of ideas and thoughts. Thus mankind owes the capacity to think to the division of human bodies into the two sexes.

The female body, then, provides the opportunity to use the will forces, which have not been incarnated into the physical body, in the consciousness through the soul. The male body, in contrast, provides the opportunity to use the non-incarnated powers of imagination consciously in the soul. Thus a female soul inhabits the male body and a male soul the female body. We use 'soul' here to include the non-physical part of the generative forces which, rejected by the physical body, come to consciousness in the astral body. Through these superfluous generative forces both soul types become receptive to fertilization through the spirit in various differing ways, which manifests itself as knowledge. At the time when human beings were still androgynous, fertilization by the spirit led to self-reproduction. Now the external participation of both sexes is required for physical reproduction. In the soul, however, fertilization by the spirit appears as our independent thinking life. In human beings today, there is still an echo of the sculpting of the body by the creative power active in the thinking in the development of the brain. The immature brain of the newborn is given its permanent shape through the learning processes of upright posture, speaking and thinking during the first years of life. The result of these learning and educational processes is reflected in the micro-architecture of the brain. They are the last remains of that human state in which the power of inner fertilization provided for the reproduction of the androgynous human being. 'This power, by which human beings form the brain with its thought processes, is the same by which human beings in ancient times fertilized themselves' (Steiner[58]). Now we are in a position to understand why Haeckel was led from his observation of embryonic development to an Imaginative form connected with the development of knowledge. It is the same material in two different guises.

This metamorphosis of the generative forces is expressed in the symbol of the snake which eats its body and turns it into light. The image is reflected in the phrase 'The "I" knows itself' (Figure 21, page 69). This expression from the mysteries refers not simply to self-knowledge in the ordinary sense.

> The concept of 'knowledge' had a much deeper, more real meaning at the time when spiritual matters were understood in a much more real sense. In the Bible it says 'And Adam knew Eve his wife' (Gen.4:1), or this or that patriarch 'knew his wife.' One does not need to be a genius to understand that this refers to procreation. And if we look at the expression 'know thyself' in Greek, then it does not mean gape inside yourself but fertilize yourself with the material which flows from the spiritual world. Know thyself means fertilize yourself with the content of the spiritual world. ... What really happens, is that the astral body makes an impression of its organs in the etheric body, with the result that human beings perceive a spiritual world surrounding them; in other words, that inwardly, in the

astral body, they receive what the etheric body has to offer, what the etheric body extracts from the cosmos, from the cosmic 'I' (Steiner[59]).

And by this means the science of the spirit has brought us back to the respiratory process in the cerebrospinal fluid, where we saw the respiration of the astral body as sensory organ for the vital motions of the etheric body which are no longer tied to the physical body.

The cause which led to the division of the sexes — the solidification of earth substance — led at an earlier stage to the separation of the sun from the earth, with which it had originally been united. At the same time the highest sun being, Christ, left the earth. He only reunited himself with the earth when the progressive hardening of human bodies began to endanger the incarnation of human beings even in their single-sex form. This renewal of the life of the earth through unificiation with the sun's Christ being began with John's baptism of Jesus in the Jordan. John the Baptist immerses the whole body of Jesus in the river. As Jesus rises from the water again, the dove as symbol of the Holy Spirit hovers above him, and the cosmic Word flowing in the etheric says: 'Thou art my beloved son! This day have I begotten thee' (Luke 3:22; Ps.2:7). The body of mankind and its life on earth was spiritually fertilized. What happened in the baptism in Jordan on a cosmic scale has its physiological equivalent in the human head. The brain, submersed in salty fluid, provides the 'I' with the physical basis for receiving the spirit from the surrounding etheric in the form of the illumination of ideas.

'Developing an awareness of ideas as they manifest themselves in reality is the true communion' (Steiner[60]). Anyone who learns such awareness through Rudolf Steiner's epistemology is able to observe the living, purposeful flow of the substance of these ideas. And they will rediscover it when they look at the existence of organisms, where in the archetype it reveals its capacity for metamorphosis in the physical world. This fluid motion of living ideas illuminates the previously obscure links between sensory facts in a way which makes the warmth of enthusiasm radiate from this light.

Thus we receive living ideas as 'light-imbued reality warmly submersing itself in the phenomena of the world. This submersion occurs through the power which flows in the active use of the thinking

itself, which is the power of love expressed in spiritual terms'
(Steiner[61]). That is how we may describe the sun-substance of the
thinking. It is conceived through respiration in the cerebrospinal fluid
and appears on an Imaginative level as religious worship in the temple
of the body. Through the act of living cognition the fertilizing baptism
by the sun spirit is consummated in the etheric.

14. The evolution of organic science

The etheric body, subject to inversion in the head by the 'I,' is the
life-form which generates concepts. In his *Philosophy of Freedom,*
Rudolf Steiner described this life-form for the first time independently
of its sensory content. The method by which he goes on to investigate
the development of the thinking and presents in *Welt- und Lebensanschauungen des 19. Jahrhunderts*[62] his results is not one commonly
employed by historians of philosophy. They look at ideas and
concepts in their historical context. Steiner immersed himself in the
thought processes of individual philosophers and observed the way
they metamorphosed from one to the next. The result bears the same
kind of relationship to the ordinary history of philosophy as Goethan-
istic organic science does to descriptive natural science. Thus he also
calls this work a 'comparative history of philosophy and its development.'[63] It is dedicated to — Ernst Haeckel! By this means Steiner set
out for Haeckel and the whole scientific community his understanding
of 'monism.' He investigated the generative forces by using the
methods of natural science also in the area where these forces arose
in the thinking consciousness. This book, too, was conceived under
the motto 'observation of the soul by scientific method.' It says about
the gastraea idea: 'It represented an idea of immense significance.' In
the book, Rudolf Steiner transforms the evolutionary theory of natural
science into one based on the science of the spirit in an inversion
process.

> I was able to understand the real development of the organic
> from primeval times up to the present on an Imaginative

level only after the work on *Welt- und Lebensanschauungen* had been completed,

he writes in his autobiography. And he continues:

> While I was doing this work, I still had the natural scientific view before my inner eye, based as it is on the Darwinian way of thinking. But to me it only represented a clearly obvious series of natural occurrences. For me, spiritual impulses were active in this series of occurrences in a similar fashion to what Goethe envisaged in his metamorphosis idea (Steiner[64]).

In the evolutionary theory which was presented in 1910 in *Occult Science, an Outline,* the 'basic law of biogenesis' is then applied to the whole of evolution: every new planetary incarnation is preceded by an abbreviated repetition of the evolutionary process to that point, so that beings can adapt to the new conditions.

> When human beings in embryonic form appeared on the new Sun, they did so first of all at the level of development which they had reached on Saturn. They had initially to transform the various developmental stages which they had passed through on Saturn so as to adapt them to the conditions prevalent on the Sun. The Sun epoch thus begins with a recapitulation of conditions on Saturn, but adapted to the changed circumstances of life on the Sun.[65]

Thus Haeckel, in making the idea of evolution an accepted part of the world view of wide circles, decisively laid the groundwork for the later work of anthroposophy in a way which has not been properly recognized. Today we can see that what is wrong in Haeckelian thinking, the inevitable result of its time, merely represents the ashes of a mighty spiritual fire which illuminated Rudolf Steiner's path. The latter liberated it from these ashes and later wrote to Edouard Schuré:

> Now, in spite of all German philosophy ... Haeckel's phylo-genetic idea is the most significant event in German intellectual life in the latter half of the nineteenth century. And there is no better scientific foundation to esotericism than Haeckel's teaching. Haeckel's teaching is exemplary, but Haeckel is the worst commentator on it.[66]

Steiner refers back to Haeckel even in the images which he uses in *Occult Science*. The latter coined the term 'morula' or 'mulberry' for the solid ball of cells which develops in the germ stage. Steiner uses the image of the 'mulberry' or 'blackberry' for the fourth stage of Saturn development as regards the configuration of the human body in the Saturn stage of the earth.

Later, in 1924, Rudolf Steiner describes the inversion process which underlay his description of evolution in *Occult Science:*

> Today, having come into contact with Rosicrucian principles of initiation in the sense referred to here, you must study Haeckel with all his materialism; you must study him and then allow the cognitive methods which are set out in *Knowledge of the Higher Worlds* to penetrate you. You should learn everything that can be learnt through natural science, even if what you learn in Haeckel's *Anthropogenie* about our human ancestors might repel you. Open that to divine influence and the result will be what my book *Occult Science* says about evolution.[67]

This opening to 'divine influence' was undertaken by Steiner, as we saw, in his work on *Welt- und Lebensanschauungen des 19. Jahrhunderts*. Goethe and Haeckel, starting from their observation of the world, had transformed the evolutionary idea into an existential force. In his own reflective activity Steiner observed the life of the world as it manifested itself in the consciousness and, ever consistent, then supplemented Goethe's and Haeckel's revolutionary ideas about the world with his 'comparative history of philosophy and its development.' With this step, natural and human development was unified in true monism. This unity appears in *Occult Science* in the chapter 'Man and the evolution of the world.' Thus it does not seem odd, but consistent when at a later date he divides the basic philosophies of mankind into twelve groups related to the zodiac, but also assigns twelve animal groups to the zodiac. They are two directions of metamorphosis arising from a single origin.[68]

Organic science thus passes through the same stages of development as the world itself. As a first step at the beginning of the modern age, the earth is understood as a sphere. Martin Behaim, for instance, constructs the first globe in Nürnberg in 1491. Physical nature is investigated and physics begins to develop. Three centuries pass until the decisive step for an understanding of living matter occurs through Goethe. The 'Copernicus and Kepler of organic science' discovers the archetypal plant in 1787. In line with earlier considerations, we may add the extended sphere as a second step on an Imaginative level here. Nearly a hundred years later, Haeckel discovers the gastraea, the archetypal animal. Steiner understands the cognitive quality of these three stages and illuminates them with the light of self-reflective thinking in his basic epistemological writings. He builds the inner bridge between Goethe and Haeckel:

> Goethe's ideas provide ... a conceptual explanation for the
> fact discovered by Darwin and Haeckel that the
> development of the individual is a recapitulation of the
> history of the species.[69]

Darwin and Haeckel discovered the 'how' of evolution, but they failed to find its subject — which is precisely Goethe's archetype. Since Haeckel did not take up the idea of the archetype, he was unable to extend his evolutionary theory to include human beings. Steiner combines the first two steps of organic science in order then to introduce the inversion process which explains the human head. Reincarnation is introduced as an evolutionary principle — something which we will discuss in greater detail below. The physiological process which we have noted as inversion in the head is a reflection of the process which takes place on a spiritual level with the whole body between death and a new birth. Inversion as the process of reincarnation becomes the physiological process of thinking in the head. On earth, true thinking is the free, creative handling of generative forces which have been liberated from the body independently of the cosmic beings which are responsible for the 'great' inversion. If human beings use these freely won Intuitions to fertilize the vital processes which are tied to the body and which underlie volition, their actions, too, will be filled with freedom. In other words, they continue the evolution of the earth with the stock of free etheric forces at their disposal. Rudolf Steiner therefore calls it ethical individualism, which he develops in his *Philosophy of Freedom,* 'the crowning glory of the building which Darwin and Haeckel sought to construct in the natural sciences. It is the spiritual manifestation of evolutionary theory applied

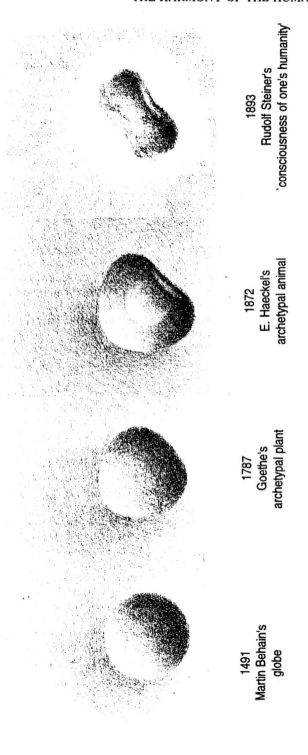

Figure 25. The development of organic science (drawings by Daniel Moreau).

to ethics.'[70] Thus we can see the developmental stages of organic science in Goethe, Haeckel and Steiner.

The gaps between the individual stages become increasingly shorter (296 years, 85 years, 19 years). If we recall the musical structure of the inversion process we will understand the dynamic which underlies this acceleration.

In order to avoid Steiner's metamorphosis of the generative forces being confused with Freud's sublimation theory, let us recall that this metamorphosis is a function of the 'I.' This means, as we explained above (page 79), that the thinking in its most vital form, which utilizes the reproductive forces in the consciousness, handles the generative forces which have been liberated from the body. Whereas in Freud the consciousness is tied to the physical subconscious, Steiner recognizes the free deed of the spirit acting of its own volition, which gradually overcomes these ties.

15. Upright posture

In the embryonic and growth stages, the musical processes of the soul body structure the sculptural stream from the outside. This can be approached musically through the proportions which can be measured externally (page 42). Its inner activity in the organs requires, in contrast, that we understand organic functions in three-dimensional and living concepts which are then placed in relation to other organic activities. Just as the astral body lives musically in the interval between two tones, so it lives physiologically in the exchange between two (or more) organic processes.

Thus we can reflect on our upright posture with concepts which are inwardly alive. We can feel what it means to stand on the ground with our two feet. The feet carry us; they have immediate sensory contact with the earth through the sense of touch. The tactual sensation of the soles transmits the feeling of pressure which is caused by our weight. This 'plinth' of the 'pillar' which is our body can then be compared with its 'capital,' the head. If we look straight ahead, we do not feel anything of the weight which the head undoubtedly possesses. The construction of the limbs, so that the head is balanced on the gravity axis, means that we do not perceive its weight. Only when the head is tilted away from that axis to the front or back, right or left, do we notice that the head also possesses physical weight. Internally, this elimination of any effect that weight might have corresponds to the buoyancy of the cerebrospinal fluid. Equally the muscles which have to deal with the laws of gravity in the feet, legs and hip joints are in a special position in the head. The extrinsic eye muscles which control where we look, turn two spheres when they turn the eyeballs. Here the centre of gravity and the pivot fall together in the same point which means that gravity has no effect on the movement of the eyes (Hollwich[71]). The eye muscles operate gravity free.

Internally, the ciliary muscles alter the curvature of the lens and thus its power of refraction·through accommodation. These muscles, then, are not affected by gravity, which has been negated in the way that the parts are arranged, but are integrated into the optical laws of light. The muscles participate in image formation since their movement determines the image on the retina and thus the image of the world which we see. We can observe here on a functional level the inversion process which we already noted embryologically: the muscles are liberated from the physical will function and integrated into a purely soul-spiritual perceptive function.

Seen from its inner psychological side, the will is present in the feet to a large degree on an unconscious, obscure level. In ordinary life, the activity of the feet takes place unnoticed and unobserved, while the will with which our hands grasp things and our eyes observe the world is brighter and more awake. In the head itself, the will provides the concepts for sensory observations through the thinking. The will which is illuminated by the bright light of consciousness — of whose Imaginative physiology we are aware — is so unlike the dark will of the limbs that we usually do not notice the activity of the will in the thinking. The latter, wholly illuminated by the 'I,' appears as the power by which we develop or originate thoughts. Mathematical reasoning refers to the steps of a proof. These are steps of the will whose content is fully transparent. Thus the same polarity is evident to inner psychological observation just as it is to outer observation, and both can be joined together. In the feet the will lives in the obscurity of the unconscious and of gravity. The feet have no sensory organs for perceiving light. The inner darkness of the will lives in the outer darkness of gravity. In the head inner light of consciousness and outer sensory light penetrate one another. Seen from the perspective of the inner sculptural exercize, we have here on an Imaginative level the polarity between the physical sphere and the light sphere which has been created through inversion.

Functionally, the brightness of thinking which shines in the head is the condition for upright posture. If we see an upright human being we know immediately that he is awake — and that means thinking actively. As soon as consciousness in the 'I' is reduced, it is no longer compatible with an upright posture, which is most clearly obvious when we faint. It is less clearly apparent in all those people for whom the full cerebral illumination of the consciousness is not possible because of illness. The result is a wandering gait and bent posture because the force which keeps the body in balance comes from the wholly awake consciousness in the 'I,' from thinking activity. In assuming an upright posture, we become aware physically of the will which lives in the thinking. In human beings, thinking takes the place of the front limbs in animals. The process which enables it to appear helps the physical body to overcome gravity — in standing upright — and functionally replaces[72] the organs which support the body of animals incapable of reflection. The circumstances which we observed on an inward level in Part One are physically evident here.

We can sum up the comparison between the activity of the feet and the head in the following way: the feet are the physical basis, the head the spiritual basis of the upright figure. In Part One we characterized the inversion processes which occur physiologically in the head as linked in musical terms to the octave. All this preliminary work was necessary in order to be able to understand a basic fact of musical physiology, which Rudolf Steiner used in referring to this field of medical research:

> Human beings know that they have the head on top and the feet below and that the two are quite different things. And anyone who undertakes a real study of the human being will find this just as important as, say, the physical descriptions

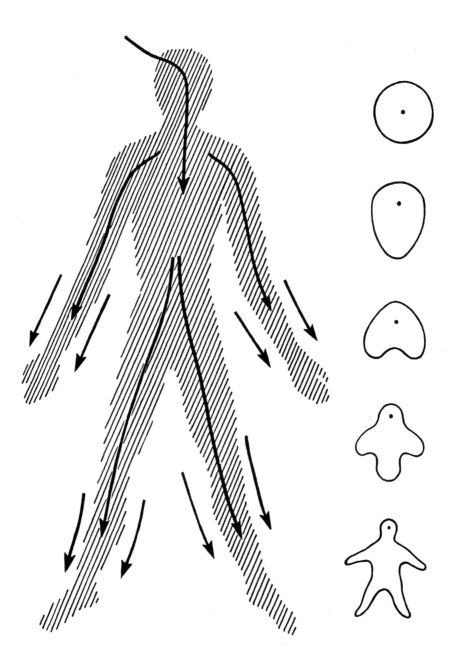

Figure 26a.

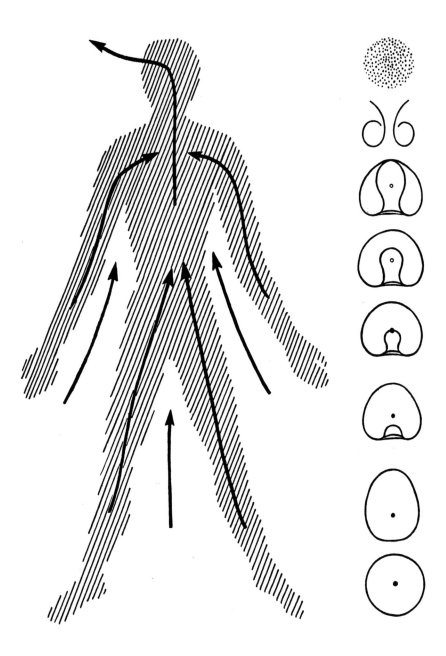

Figure 26b.

in anatomy of the heel bone, the phalanges, the metatarsus
and so on in the foot, of the parietal, frontal, occipital
bones and so on in the head. Moving inside, we come to
descriptions of the brain. Then the muscles of the foot are
described. All these things are referred to as if someone
had assembled them in an arbitrary fashion with a result
that just happened to be the human form. In reality the head
forms the octave of the foot. And this is just as much of a
reality as the things which can be found in anatomy books.
For if you examine the action of the feet and proceed from
there to the contribution which the head makes to it —
and the head does have something to do with the fact that
you can walk with the feet — and if you really understand
the activity of the head and of the feet, then you will get
an exact feeling of the relationship between the former
and the latter from the way that the octave relates to the
prime.[73]

All the intervals with the exception of the octave contain something
vibrant or dammed up, something searching which intensifies into
longing; in short, they contain desire in one form of metamorphosis
or another. Only the octave is completely free of it and in its purity
transmits the most comprehensive musical richness. The transcendence
of the weight of matter by the thinking in the etheric is based on the
transcendence of the desires in the astral, as can be experienced in the
approach to the octave and in the latter itself. When and at what stage
in life this transcendence takes place will be discussed later when we
examine the question of when and why the inversion process is
activated in the head in the first place.

The inner sculptural exercise discloses an Imaginative physiology
of the thinking. It enables us to understand the development of organic
science and the physiology of the liquor system. The external limb
exercise leads us to the opposite end of the human structure. With this
part of the etheric body human beings enter and comprehend the
external physical world. This exercise explains the human growth
processes. The measurement of eight times head height which can be
taken from the outside is accompanied by eight inner, organic
functional areas which adjoin one another as locomotory apparatus and

body cavities: 1. the feet; 2. the lower leg; 3. the thigh; 4. the pelvis; 5. the abdomen; 6. the thorax; 7. the neck; 8. the head.

Just as the limb exercise incorporates the sculptural, incarnating stream, so the inversion exercise represents the excarnating musical one. In the first instance, we will compare hypothetically its eight stages with the eight inner functional areas. We have already examined the activity of the feet and the head as the prime and the octave of the musical stream. We now have to look at the remaining organic functions in respect of their musical qualities.

16. Germ cell formation, fertilization and pregnancy

From the prime connected with the activity of the feet, we reach the pelvic zone with step four, the fourth, if we take Figure 26b hypothetically as our guide. Above it lies the abdominal area as the region of the fifth. The pelvis has a lower part (the so-called 'true pelvis') and an upper basin-shaped section with which it opens to the abdominal cavity. Thus we need to examine the extent to which the male germ cells are formed in the forces of the fourth and the female germ cells in the forces of the fifth. How would this be expressed sculpturally in anatomical terms?

The prime of the feet rests on the ground in surface contact with the forces which radiate from the centre of the earth. The head exists in the inversion zone of the octave where the cosmic etheric forces penetrate through the physical cerebrospinal fluid. The fifth is affected by this vortex to the extent that under its influence the female germ cell in the region of the fifth expands as it matures into a sphere of a size which makes it the only cell in the human body which can just be seen with the bare eye. In contrast, the male sperm cell loses its plasma covering as it matures. The representative of the point-forces in the cell, the nucleus, is the only thing that remains, and it too becomes still denser so that it becomes increasingly opaque under the microscope (Benninghoff[74]). We see the powers of compression of the fourth in the histological image of the maturing sperm. The uterus receives the egg cell from the region of the fifth and the sperm cell from the region of the fourth. As we saw in our examination of the growing embryo (compare page 27), the mother receives the new human being from two directions:

— from the cosmos come all those things built up in the past which are wholly stored in the head;

— from the father come those forces which enable the human being to find his footing on earth in view of his future development, and which sculpt the rest of the body out of the head.

When the arms hang down loosely, the wrists are positioned at the level where we find the fourth as far as the function of the internal organs are concerned: at the level of the male gonads. But according to spiritual scientific research, the wrists are also the region where the fourth comes to expression in terms of the representation of the intervals in eurythmy (see page 220). Suchantke and Pracht found the fourth to be active in the carpal bones, a finding based on the morphological impression of the interruption and damming up of the skeletal structure in the arm in the carpus, as well as in the fact that these bones only begin to ossify after birth. They therefore need physical conditions to give them their form. Moreover, Suchantke and Pracht refer to the phenomenon connected with the fourth that the ossification period of the carpal bones only comes to an end with puberty, that is, in the period of when physical reproduction becomes possible.[75]

The character of the fourth is illuminated by the fact that processes which can be interpreted in musical terms from a great variety of perspectives intersect as they meet in the fourth. The perspective which demonstrates the effect of the fourth in the newborn (temporal proportion 1/3:1/4) is something quite different from the one which leads to the fourth being found in the reproductive organs of the body. That is different again from the presentation of the intervals in the arms in eurythmy. In no other interval so far have we found this phenomenon of the intersection of various perspectives.

Thus the 'octave of reproduction' which we found at the beginning through external measurement appears here again, but this time it is formed through the power of the fourth in the father and the power of the fifth in the mother.

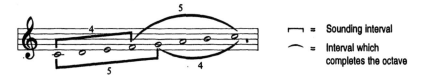

Example 10.

This is the physiology of the inner emptiness and openness which is produced by the octave. We experience musically the negative aspect of the fourth, its hollowness. That is also why the fourth and the fifth can be transformed from one to the other in the octave like positive and negative. The interval which completes the octave from the fourth is the fifth. If we move on to the fifth from the fourth, then the octave is completed by the fourth. When the fourth moves to the fifth it enters its own completion interval, something which none of the other intervals can do with their adjacent ones. The compression of the fourth is followed in the next step by the emptiness of the fifth, rather like entering the cavity which the fourth has left as an impression of its form.

This loosening reflects the soul state of the mother-to-be, living in an enhanced state of awareness as if in a protective sphere outside the body. It is the soul state of the fifth. The pregnant woman is taken back into a state which was common to mankind in earlier times. For human beings, before they became at home in the third as they are today, experienced this state when the fifth sounded: 'The music of the fifth made people feel that they were taken out of themselves' (Steiner[76]).

The fifth occupies an unstable position between the basic forces of the prime and the bright forces of the octave. It has left the region where the prime is active and has touched on the region of the octave.

In the limb system there is further evidence of this unstable intermediary position of the fifth, in that the body's centre of gravity when we stand or walk is situated above the support axis which is vital for upright posture. This axis passes through the two hip joints in the region of the fourth. The centre of gravity lies in the central

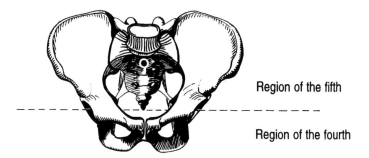

Region of the fifth

Region of the fourth

Figure 27. The position of the body's centre of gravity (●) above the support axis of the hip joints in a person standing upright (after Benninghoff-Goerttler).

axis some three to five centimetres above the plane of the hip joints, approximately at the level of the third sacral vertebra.[77] This means that the body's centre of gravity in the upright person is in an unstable position, that is, it tries, in so far as it is subject to the laws of mechanics, to reposition itself below the support axis. In other words, in order to maintain an upright posture human beings need another force to counter the mechanics of gravity. As we saw, the attainment of upright posture is not something which has a mechanical basis but it lives in the will forces of the thinking. But this will force remains awake and active only for as long as it is aroused by a perception. Such a perception is represented by the unstable position of the centre of gravity, that is, the inherent tendency of the mechanical system to seek to reposition the centre of gravity below the support axis. The will in the muscles experiences this instability in the form of the fifth.

Exposed to the cosmos in this way, the female organization has the tendency to withdraw from the forces contained in the fourth. The malformation of the hip joints such that the sockets in the hip bone are too flat and the head of the thigh bone slides up into the region of the fifth from the fourth is four to eight times more common in girls than in boys (congenital dislocation of the hip).

In the octave (of the head), the overall experience of the will which is present in upright posture is brought musically to consciousness. In the fifth, the will is experienced in the power to stand upright at the point in the body where this power originates. The cerebrospinal fluid connected with the octave just extends in its furthest reaches into the region of the fifth where the spinal column ends at the level of the third coccygeal vertebra. This is the inner anatomical arrangement of the living relationship between the forces contained in the octave and their physical contact point in the region of the fifth. For upright posture human beings receive the will forces of their own higher self from the octave of the head. They direct the body towards its cosmic origins. In the region of the fifth, where the centre of gravity is balanced, the mother also receives the will forces of the higher self of the child from the octave of its head, which rays from the cosmos into the sphere of the fifth as its spiritual embryo.

The threefold etheric human being stands before us, alternating between the fifth in the waters of reproduction and the fluidity of conceptual illumination in the area where the octave applies. The region of the fifth in the body is thus doubly receptive: from the octave of the archetypal sphere of the spiritual embryo, the willing-ness to be connected with the earth flows in through outside fertiliza-tion. From the octave of the body's own head flows the urge to be free of the earth, which comes through self-fertilization in the living idea.

17. The formation of words

We can now compare the region of the fourth more closely with the region of the seventh. The major seventh owes its quality to the fact that it has moved very far out of the sphere of influence of the prime on the one hand, while on the other hand the power of the octave exerts a strong influence on it, literally drawing it upwards. The sepa-ration of only a semi-tone from a tone which itself remains unheard (the octave) powerfully influences the seventh so that it is continually 'on the wing to the octave.'

If we recall the figure of the octave, it is clear that any connection with heaviness, matter, weight — or, on a soul level, desire of any sort — disappears when the breakthrough to the octave occurs. The function of the associated organ in the service of the physical and mineral body would have to be transformed into a spiritual function in the upward movement. This happens, as we have already mentioned, in the larynx and its association with the lung. The air exhaled from the metabolism is inverted into the octave of the word through the power of the seventh. The extreme agitation with which the seventh shimmers can be found in the larynx where the most rapid and most active muscular activity in the body takes place. In accordance with the semi-tone between the seventh and the octave this function should be connected with compression. The compression of the air is manifest physically in the muscles of the glottis.

The sounding expiratory air flow is formed into vowels through muscles which start at the head. The seventh receives the sculpted forms of the consonants, created by the reproduction of sensory perceptions, from the region of the octave in the head. Thus in the musical structure of human beings the word is produced in the step from the seventh to the octave. The octave of the head is joined by the octave of the word. In examining the inversion process (see page 67) we had already come to understand the word as 'the attempt in the medium of air to form a head.' In the activity of the lungs and the larynx, the metabolic process connected with the air is overcome in its physical function and formed into a manifestation of the spirit, the word. The male part of the reproductive organs, which compresses the germ cells through the work of the fourth, creates what its own nature dictates according to its function: the physical body. In opposition to the larynx, the reproductive organ adheres to its own physical nature. The fourth is the interval of hereditary functions. The step from the seventh to the octave is the interval of language functions.

18. Standing and walking

Let us think of the key-note as the prime when we stand upright and at rest. It is active in the calm, supporting strength of the feet with the weight evenly distributed between them.

Example 11.

What happens musically when we move to stage two with the second? Solid rest is transformed into movement through the slight rise in tone. Rest becomes fluid. The second is the step by which the incarnated 'I' moves in music today in creating the diatonic scale. The calf muscle traverses the knee joint and the ankle joint. By this means it bends the knee and 'allows us to rise to our toes and lift the foot in walking, running and jumping' (Benninghoff-Goerttler[78]). Our sensation in the raised foot consists of the disappearance of body weight, which was carried by the pillar of the lower leg when in the prime position. It is transformed into a feeling of the weight of the lower leg and the foot themselves which is now being carried.

Tonic-prime feeling: 'I rest my weight on my feet.'

Second feeling: 'I carry the weight of my lower leg and foot.' The step from the prime to the second is the step from a feeling of unity with the force of gravity to a feeling of one's own weight as something external which can be moved. We liberate ourselves from the force of gravity in the second.

In the sculptural and artistic context we find this step in the development of Greek sculpture. In the archaic period the legs of the statues rest in the prime position like pillars. Then the moment arrives when in the classical period the 'free leg' is lifted and the whole sculpture awakens to life. This is due physiologically to the fact that in lifting the leg a wealth of connected movements are triggered in the whole body. The interplay of compensatory movements in the hips, spine, neck, shoulders and arms (Figures 28 and 29) is set in motion.

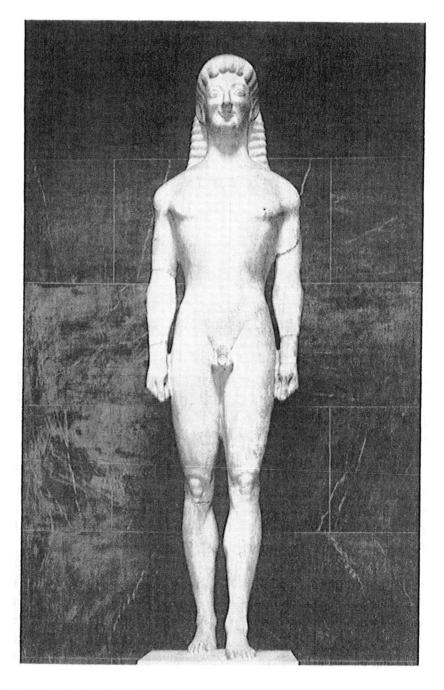

Figure 28. Apollo of Tenea (c. 600 BC): prime (tonic)

Figure 29. Doryphoros *by Polycletus (c. 450 BC): second (step two)*

On the basis of the inner exercise, which we related to the eight head heights and the eight functional areas, we should now examine the third in the thigh. Its movement involves muscles which are no longer purely external. The power which flexes the hip joint comes largely from a muscle which reaches outwards from the inside of the body (m. iliopsoas). Originating in the transverse processes of the lumbar spinal column, it stretches along the posterior wall of the abdominal cavity into the pelvis, exits from the groin and is attached to the thigh bone. The flexion of the thigh is thus a movement which continues into the internal space of the body and can be compared with the transition from the second to the third. (The relationship between the classification of intervals here and the one which is given for the legs in music eurythmy is discussed in Part Four).

The hypothetical relationship between the inversion exercise and the musical stream from the feet into the head (see Figure 26b) has thus been confirmed for the prime, fourth, fifth, seventh and octave, and for the third in outline. The sixth has to remain a theoretical consideration for reasons to do with the sculptural process itself, because the thinning of a three-dimensional form into a 'transparent membrane' goes beyond our three-dimensional experience. At this point we cease our observation of the etheric because the whole process comes under the influence of the astral sphere. Physically, the musical stream from the feet into the region of the head is accompanied by the venous blood. In the lower tetrachord (= intervals from the prime to the fourth), it flows first in the legs which are dominated by external forces. Then the venous blood unites with the rich internal life of the abdominal organs. Now the inferior vena cava, which has received the blood from all the parts of the body below the diaphragm, passes through a gap in the latter. The blood reaches the right side of the heart and from there flows into the lung. In Part One we saw this process musically as the transformation of the minor stream into the major stream in the heart. With this step the blood leaves the heart and flows into the thin membrane of the alveoli in the lungs. They have a huge surface area of approximately seventy square metres, and it is through them that it can use the surrounding air for respiration. If we follow the course of the venous blood from the prime of the feet to the way it is externalized in the respiratory process, we find the

major sixth in its real, living activity. The sculptural borderline
experience was only a weak shadow of this ('internal space unites in
a single point with external space'). The major sixth is preceded by
the more internal minor sixth in the collection of the blood in the right
side of the heart.

Later on we will encounter the processes connected with the fifth
and the major third in the surface physiology of the lung. The function
of the intervals in relation to the body is always connected with a
specific reference point because it is that relationship which defines
the process. After all, the underlying nature of music consists precisely
in the fact that one and the same note can be simultaneously a third
for example (in relation to the key-note), a sixth, fifth and seventh (in
its relationships to other notes sounding at the same time). If it is
reached by the step of a second, the single note contains the qualities
of the second, third, fourth, sixth and seventh all intermingling. Thus
we have to think of every organ as containing a symphonic totality of
musical forces. But our cognition can only function step by step, in
stages.

If this is the way that the forces of the intervals work in the human
being, then we should also discover these generative impulses, as we
have described them, where, liberated from the body, they are active
in the musical creativity of a composer. A good example of this is the
theme of Mozart's Sonata in A major, K. 331:

Example 12.

Essentially, the melody in the first eight bars keeps within the lower tetrachord, that is, it does not go beyond the fourth. Then it rises (from bar nine) from the fifth to the sixth, swings more urgently up to the seventh and octave, only to return in cadences to the lower tetrachord. The style of the movement alters noticeably, when the melody enters the sphere of the fifth and moves within the upper tetrachord. The accompanying chordal harmonies turn into a flowing legato; we are suddenly transposed from a static, internally tied gesture into a flowing force-field which is melodically set in motion by the accompaniment. Thus we can see in the sculptural structuring of the musical form the metamorphosis of what we observed as the physiological effect in the human being. The example of Beethoven on page 79 shows the one-sided way in which this flow is concentrated on the seventh since here we are dealing with a final movement.

Following this investigation of musical physiology, we can now answer a question which remained unanswered in Chapter 2 (see page 31: Why is it that the 'musical stream' from below upwards initially accompanies the venous blood, but then changes to the arterial blood which flows in the carotid artery as it moves on upwards with exhalation? The venous blood flows in the opposite direction down from the head in the veins of the neck! The reversal occurs above the heart where the superior vena cava leads into the heart. From a purely musical perspective, after the sixth the astral body encounters an opposing stream coming from the octave. (At the fifth there is already an awareness that this flow exists, as we saw. But this awareness as yet has no specific quality and remains indeterminate.) This is reflected on a physical level in the veins flowing in the opposite direction, in the transformation of the relationship between the musical motion and the blood flow. It is already signalled in the inversion of the blood into cerebrospinal fluid in the head.

Figure 30 shows the morphology of the 'I' and of growth in terms of their musical structures. The eightfold division of the 'I' thus arises from three perspectives which are totally independent of one another:

1. Through measuring proportions (see Figure 6, page 26);
2. Through the functions of the body (see Figure 26b, page 93);
3. Through the stages of the inversion exercise (see Figure 22, page 70).

Thus these processes support one another and verify the cognitive value of the artistic qualities.

19. The octave of the head and of the word

In conclusion, let us look once more at language formation in order to understand the relationship between the octave of the word and the octave of the head. The ash produced by our body is expelled through respiration, getting rid of the surplus carbon dioxide which would otherwise poison us. In the lungs, the carbon dioxide leaves the blood in the form of a volatile gas and rises up through the bronchi and the trachea. Almost at the point where it leaves the body, the larynx intervenes. It shuts the windpipe tightly. The exhaled air is dammed and warms up as pressure increases. Then the glottis opens and the air slides past the vibrating vocal cords like a bow slides over the strings of a violin. The vehicle of the body's residues is transformed into sound. The sounding air flows into the 'consonant workshop' of the head and is sculpted into the word in the fluidity of the saliva. The 'I' transforms the dead body into the meaningful sounds of language; it guides physical life through death and forms a new body of the word with the spiritual life of the thinking. The product of the physical body, which in the form of ash heads towards excretion through the lung in the venous blood and is inverted into the musical life of the word, is the result of our active will in the body; for it is the end product of the metabolic process.

What archetypal image do human beings reflect when they speak? We will find the answer if we imagine the partial dying of the body radically extended into full death. Once the soul has shed the etheric body as well, it rises through its time of purification into the musical life of the cosmic harmonies of the spheres. Finally, it reaches the sphere of the cosmic word at the cosmic midnight hour. There the results of its deeds in its past life are recast through divine action into the plan which will be its destiny in the next life. The limbs and torso of the previous life — their soul and spiritual equivalent in the spiritual world — undergo an inversion process to become what will be the head in the next life.

The human being's head is the word with which the higher self, breathing in the rhythm of its incarnations, expresses itself out of the cosmic word. Physical speech, as image of this cosmic process, provides the starting point for forming a new head out of the dying substance of the physical body; it is the attempt to realize in the present on a microcosmic level what will happen in the future macrocosmically after death. We recall: 'Human language is the persistent attempt of the larynx in the medium of air to become head.'

In the word, the 'I' creates a musical image of its future incarnation. In the head, the 'I' lives in the sculptural image of its past life on earth. In between these two forms it breathes in the present. With this we return to the two images from Part One (Figures 8 and 26).

Thus we have won a new point of departure from which we can reflect on the octave at a higher level. Until now we have concentrated primarily on the new elements which occur in the octave when compared with the prime. But if we are aware that we hear the same note in the octave as in the prime we will be able to experience the following: 'I can hear in my head the note connected with the activity of my feet. Do I not experience the tonic of my foot activity on a higher level?' The tension between the inner, heavy, opaque point of rest of the tonic and the luminous octave of the head, in which we saw the spiritual basis for upright posture, leads to the image of a

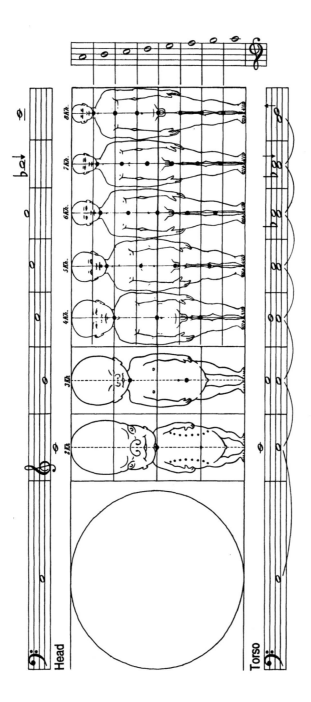

Figure 30. The morphology of the 'I' and of growth in sculptural and musical terms.

spiritualized foot activity in the head. It is based on the inversion of the limbs into the head as explained above. A full experience of the octave, which mankind will only achieve in the future, will reveal the word of the octave to be something along the following lines: 'I am here for the second time.' The octave will become the musical expression of reincarnation in that human beings will experience that they, together with spiritual beings, have formed their heads from the strides which their feet took in their previous lives on earth. Those strides became their speech movements when they were united with the beings of the creative cosmic word. If their present strides on earth reach fulfilment in the cognitive illumination of their heads, as the prime reaches fulfilment in the octave, then human beings will create harmony between these strides on earth and the destiny which speaks in their higher self, that is, the will of the gods.

> Then the experience of music will become proof of the existence of God because human beings will have a twofold experience of the 'I.' Once as the physical internal 'I' and the other time as a spiritual, external 'I.' And when the octave is used in the same general way as sevenths, fifths or thirds — the octave is not yet used like that today — then that will be a new way of proving the existence of God. For that is the way that the octave will be experienced. People will say: If I experience my 'I' on one level as it is on earth, in the prime, and then experience it again as it is in the spirit, then this is the inner proof of the existence of God. ... and that will result in human beings feeling the musical scale to be a part of themselves, and they will feel themselves to be inhabiting both worlds (Steiner[79]).

The following chapters of this Part will investigate the various organic processes in the neck and the head to discover how the forces of the seventh and the octave are manifest in this region.

20. The musical physiology of the thyroid gland and the parathyroid glands

20.1 The characteristics of dual organs

The horseshoe-shaped thyroid gland is situated below the larynx at the front of the trachea. The parathyroid glands — four lens-sized epithelial bodies — lie behind the thyroid gland. Both organs thus lie within the inversion zone of the etheric body.

The thyroid gland and the parathyroid glands form a dual structure which also occurs in the anatomy of other organs in human beings. Kidneys/adrenal glands, liver/gall bladder, inner ear/organ of equilibrium, exocrine and endocrine pancreas, that is, external (digestion) and internal (insulin) secretions of the pancreas from the two sections of the organ, are further examples. The characteristics of these dual organs are best illustrated in the cardio-pulmonary system. The nature of such dual organs lies in one of them being oriented towards the inner body whereas the other is oriented towards the outside:

inner orientation	outer orientation
heart	lungs
adrenal gland	kidneys
liver	gall bladder
insulin cells	exocrine pancreas
organ of equilibrium	ear
parathyroid glands	thyroid glands

Many things to do with the functional relationship between the two single organs are still unclear in these dual structures. But the characteristics described above give some indication of the direction to pursue.

With regard to the thyroid gland and the parathyroid glands, the dual organ characteristics reveal the following: the human being undergoes degenerative processes in two directions. Externally all over the body through the cornified layer on the skin's surface as well as the hair and nails, and internally in the mineralization of the skeletal system. These two degenerative processes were described by Rudolf Steiner for the first time as the two sides of the 'silicic acid organism.'[80]

The symptoms which occur with subnormal or overactivity in the thyroid gland demonstrate its role in the degenerative processes at the periphery of the body:

hypothyroidism (= subnormal activity)	*hyperthyroidism* (= overactivity)
coarse, thick, dry skin	delicate, thin, sweaty skin
small eyes	protruding eyes
slowed, deep speech	excited, fast speech
constipation	diarrhoea
bradycardia (slowing of the pulse)	tachycardia (increased pulse rate)
tiredness, apathy	nervousness
no tremor	tremor (trembling of the fingers)

These opposing symptoms show the following: the overactivity of the thyroid gland means that too much vitality flows to the periphery of the body. The clearest sign of this is damp, warm and thin skin, also referred to as 'baby skin.' The subnormal activity of the thyroid gland allows too little blood to flow to the periphery and the human being appears increasingly as if encased 'by tree bark.' The degenerative matter is not removed but remains fixed.

The task which the thyroid gland performs externally is undertaken by the parathyroid glands in respect of the internal degenerative processes, the mineralization of the skeleton. Their overactivity is expressed in a higher level of bone disintegration. The healthy balance between mineralized calcium in the skeleton and soluble calcium in the blood has been disturbed in the direction of the latter. The extra calcium and phosphate which has been removed from the bones is excreted through the kidneys.[81] The parathyroid glands ensure, then, that the human being does not die off too much internally in the skeleton. They lead the bones back from their dead, mineral state towards the vital processes. They do that by facilitating the dissolution of the calcium. With overactivity of the parathyroid glands human beings thus literally lose their skeletons through the kidneys. Their subnormal activity, in contrast, leads to tetany and too high a level of mineralized calcium.

20.2 Thyroid gland and larynx

The effect of the underactivity of the thyroid gland on the sound of the voice belongs to the most marked symptoms of this illness. The sound not only deepens, but becomes rough and loses its modulation. The changes to the skin also affect the surface of the vocal cords.[82] In addition, macroglossia (an abnormally large tongue) often develops.[83] This spoils the articulation of consonants to a large degree, as can be experienced in patients with serious hypothyroidism: deep, rough, monotonous, slow, unarticulated speech. On the other hand it was found that 'singers with high, brilliant and strong voices often displayed a slight degree of overactivity in the thyroid gland' (Brodnitz[84]).

Thus we can see a functional relationship between the thyroid gland and the larynx and tongue in so far as the healthy sound of the voice, as well as the necessary mobility and slimness of the tongue to articulate consonants, are related to its functioning normally. We can understand why Rudolf Steiner called the thyroid gland a 'degenerated speech brain.'[85]

If we combine this with the image we have developed of the action of the seventh in the larynx, we can recognize the pathological effect of the overactivity of the seventh in a patient with an overactive thyroid gland. We see a person with restless, hurried speech, who sweats, has a rapid pulse and glittering, protruding eyes as well as slightly trembling finger tips.

We see here in increased metabolic activity (raised basal metabolic rate), which pushes to the outside in the blood through the skin, what in its healthy state turns into sound in the larynx through increased muscular activity. The seventh-related process in the larynx can find resolution in the octave through the consonants which form the word. Hyperthyroidism represents a surfeit of these seventh processes spread over the peripheral areas of the body; illness results because resolution in the octave is impossible by this route.

Once again we come across a passage on music by Rudolf Steiner which describes the physiological effect of this interval:

> Whereas the fifth is experienced on the surface of the skin, giving a person a full experience of himself, the seventh makes him feel as if he passes through his skin and into his environment. He feels as if he has left himself and exists in his environment.[86]

20.3 The musical physiology of the parathyroid glands

Is the seventh also active in the parathyroid glands? In order to answer this question, we have to understand the basic character of the seventh by looking at its effects in the various manifestations which we have studied so far. In one organ, in which the seventh plays a decisive role, the physical and mineral body is led to assume higher functions through inversion. The parathyroid hormone causes the mineralized bone to dissolve again. Bones which have died through the action of hydroxyapatite (calcium phosphate) are revitalized through the action of the parathyroid glands. Thus the latter transmit those forces which overcome death in the human being. They thereby demonstrate the basic character of the seventh in achetypal form: the mineral element is dissolved and abandons its crystalline form so that it can enter the higher plane of living matter.

The transcendence of death: that is the inner revelation of the word which has been incarnated in human beings. As far as the structure of the thyroid gland and the parathryroid glands is concerned, the character of dual organs results, then, in an internal and external orientation of the forces of the seventh in human beings.

| | | thyroid gland: | External aspect of the word as sound and articulation of language |
| seventh | | parathyroid glands: | Internal aspect of the word as the transcendence of death in the skeleton. |

Each of the basic physical states — solid, fluid, gaseous and heat — requires a different level of intensity to make the transition to a living state. Since heat is the physical state nearest to the spiritual one, it requires less vitality than gases or fluids, whose greater density calls for an equivalent increase in vital intensity, if they are to take on a living form. In order to prevent a form like the skeleton, which approaches the density of dead mineral matter, from dropping out of the living human framework altogether, the highest form of the etheric, the life-ether, is required.[87]

Musically, the relationship between the basic physical states and the etheric types can be seen if we observe the way in which the diatonic scale is stretched out between two poles. The intervals from the prime to the fourth are, each in their own way, related to the tonic like to a physical gravitational point. It is the same quality of the tonic which can be experienced in the feet supporting the body's weight as they rest on the ground. On the other hand the intervals of the sixth and the seventh are related to the octave such that they move towards it. This is a curious state of affairs because the octave affects the sixth and the seventh as reference note without sounding physically. Physically, we hear in the sixth or seventh the notes of the tonic and the upper sixth or seventh. In the soul, we experience the interval. But on a spiritual level the octave is active in this upper range of the scale as the reference note in polar opposition to the tonic; and it happens in a way that makes us feel drawn to this (non-sounding) tone. We feel filled with the light of the octave in the sixth and the seventh so that it makes us merge with the octave itself. The octave skims the fifth externally, but the inner experience is missing as yet. The octave

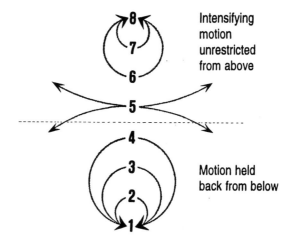

Intensifying
motion
unrestricted
from above

Motion held
back from below

Figure 31.

affects the fifth sufficiently, however, to balance the 'pull of gravity' of the prime. This results is the fifth's state of equilibrium whose physiology has already been discussed.

The stages from the prime to the fourth are therefore struggling to liberate themselves from the weight of gravity. From the fifth onwards the quality of the scale changes completely and is oriented towards the octave in liberated and intensified motion. That is the essential polarity of the scale: motion held back from below changes in the fifth into intensifying motion unrestricted from above (Figure 31).

We can see now how the intervals are related to the basic etheric states in the following way: from the fourth to the fifth we experience the change from the basic physical states into the etheric ones, the gradual transformation of form into movement (Figure 32). Rudolf Steiner wrote above this figure in his notebook:[88] 'Solid form —

solid   = *c*
fluid   = *d*
gaseous = *e*
           f
           g light ether
           a chemical ether
           b life ether

Figure 32.

transformation — dissolution of form.' The qualities of the intervals provide a classic example of the way in which the arts can help our cognition to make its own supersensory observations. Every musician 'knows' these experiences. What needs to be done is to turn this experience of supersensory reality into cognition through precise concepts.

The seventh works externally in the larynx and the thyroid gland so that it turns the physical body inside out to transform it into the sound body of the word. The seventh works internally through the parathyroid glands in overcoming death in the skeleton, dissolving the solid form. It uses these two organs to bring to reality from two sides the word living in human beings.

20.4 The overactivity of the parathyroid glands

Every art has limits to what it can represent. Music eurythmy has reached its limit when it seeks to present chords. This is connected with the fact that music eurythmy with its etheric foundation threatens to become unartistic — or physical — at the point where music becomes physical. And music becomes physical in the chords.

> ... if you experience this properly you will realize that
> chords really contain a burial — that is expressed somewhat
> radically — but each chord really contains a burial. The
> three notes which are to sound at the same time, which thus
> require space and not time in order to work, these three
> notes have died in the chord. They only live when they
> occur in a tune.[89]

Rudolf Steiner drew the relevant conclusion in the above-mentioned notebook for this lecture: 'Chords cannot be fully performed in eurythmy.'

The opposite limit of music eurythmy is reached with the presentation of the seventh. The agility with which the life of melody sweeps through the human being reaches a degree which gives the observer the feeling that here, too, eurythmy has reached a limit. For the etheric ends also at this point, as Figure 32 demonstrates.

Figure 33. Eurythmy gesture of the seventh. (Daniel Moreau).

It is characteristic of this gesture that the seventh shimmers through the human being right into the fingertips (see Figure 33). The artistic eye can see the seventh effervescing between the fingers and creating a whirling shimmer. If we compare this image with the internal function of the seventh in the body — bone calcium dissolving life ether — we will recognize the following X-ray picture (Figure 34) as something which, as doctors, we could predict through eurythmy. It is the hand of a patient suffering from overactivity of the parathyroid

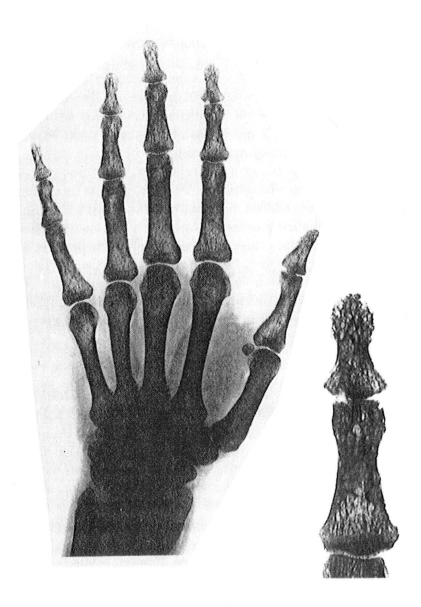

Figure 34. X-ray picture of the left hand of a patient with hyperparathyroidism. The disintegration of the bone at the end joints of the fingers can be clearly seen; alongside is an enlargement of the index finger.

glands. Characteristic symptom of this illness is the peripheral disintegration of the finger bones immediately below the periosteum. These 'subperiostal erosions' of the fingers are one of the typical characteristics of the overactivity of the parathyroid glands.

The physiology of the parathyroid glands as understood from a musical perspective creates the convergence between the eurythmy gesture of the seventh and the X-ray picture showing the results of hyperparathyroidism. The X-ray shows the physical result of the etheric forces which eurythmy makes visible.

In the light of the dual organ characteristics, the thyroid gland reveals the external manifestation of the same process here too: whereas in hyperparathyroidism the hands remain still but are subject to the internal dissolution process — which in its advanced stages affects the whole skeleton — the patient suffering from hyperthyroidism displays trembling fingers as the immediate external manifestation of the process connected with the seventh. The disintegration of the end joints of the fingers has its external equivalent to the extent that with long-term hyperthyroidism the disintegration of the fingernails (onycholysis) is a chacteristic symptom.[90]

20.5 The underactivity of the parathyroid glands (tetany) and hyperventilation tetany

With the subnormal activity of these organs, more calcium is deposited in the bones through underactivity of the life ether than is taken back into life. The bones attract too much of the calcium which reaches the blood from the food in the intestine. The level of dissolved, living calcium in the blood is thus reduced. This produces hypersensitivity in the nerves, leading in turn to a tightening of the muscles, to cramps. Depending on the type of underactivity this can take various forms. In its generalized manifestation toddlers and infants can suffocate from glottal cramps.[91]

But such cramps can also be triggered by something quite different. Certain people with a predisposition to hysteria (predominantly women) breathe much faster due to mental tension based on a more or less consciously experienced, egocentrically-oriented fear. The nervous system extends from the head into the rhythmical system of the middle through respiration. The tension which continues from the astral body into the accelerated breathing thus leads to a 'distension' of nervous activity. The patient breathes more rapidly than is appropriate for the activity of the limbs. Because in the process nervous activity extends too far into the limbs the muscles freeze into cramp-like rigidity. This makes sense of Rudolf Steiner's findings, according to which neural substance is continually in the process of ossification, that is, in a state of bone formation which has been arrested *in statu nascendi*.[92] If the nervous system comes to expression in this way, as in the spasms caused by tetany, then the character of neural substance can be felt and seen in the hardening of the limbs.

The factor which is common both to psychogenic hyperventilation tetany and tetany caused by the underactivity of the parathyroid glands is the deficiency of dissolved, ionized blood calcium. In the latter illness the death process in the bones seizes the calcium in the blood because the life ether does not provide a sufficient balance. In psychogenic tetany the respiration which is over-dominated by nervous and sensory impulses seizes the blood calcium in its dissolved state and turns it into salt through excessive carbon dioxide expiration.

The tendency towards the apparent purely 'psychogenic' hyperventilation tetany can also be due to a latent underactivity of the parathyroid glands.[93] On the other hand an important special form of hypoparathyroidism — pseudohypoparathyroidism — reveals an excessive nervous influence in skeletal development: Here calcium is deposited in the subcutaneous fatty tissue.[94] What appears in psychogenic hyperventilation tetany as a hardening of the muscles, is intensified here into a kind of 'calcium shell' around the limbs. The tendency of nervous influences to form an external skeleton as happens in the head becomes apparent.

Let us now look at the form in which the limbs harden with hyperventilation tetany. A characteristic position of the hands occurs, the so-called *main d'accoucheur* (Figure 35).

How can we understand the forces active here from a musical perspective?

How is the psychological gesture of inner egocentric hardening expressed in musical terms? In the series of intervals, the free, internally

Figure 35. Spasm caused by tetany (main d'accoucheur).

harmonious soul vibration of the third densifies with the step to the fourth. We may recall that the fourth and the seventh represent opposing forces of densification and dissolution of the physical body. The fourth is attached to the densified physical reflection of the 'I.' On page 96 we saw the correspondence between the fourth in the reproductive region and in the wrist area. It is here that the eurythmist forms the fourth. This creates a posture which has a tendency to solidification in which the fingers close up (Figure 36). In this movement we see the same impulse at work as in the characteristic motion when tetany occurs, but only, to use Schiller's words, in free play and not as painful necessity.

As in the gesture of the seventh, the common feature of art and illness becomes clear: Both reveal otherwise hidden characteristics of human beings. Through the control of his 'I,' the artist wakens and handles those processes in freedom which affect the sick person because his 'I' has lost its equilibrium of forces. This is particularly evident in the fourth and the seventh because the 'I' is affected in the relationship with its most intimate organ, the skeleton. Adherence to its internal mineral support — overcoming the mineral element: that is the activity of the 'I' in the skeleton.

Figure 36. Eurythmy gesture of the fourth (drawing by Daniel Moreau).

20.6 *The seventh as the generative power in a work of music (Chopin's Étude in C minor, Op. 10, No. 12)*

> Aesthetics is nothing more than the science of art. It reveals
> the laws which drive the artist, of which he might not even
> be aware, like the plant knows nothing of the laws of
> botany (Steiner[95]).

The creative powers which the musician has at his disposal are no
different from those which are at work in all other processes active in
the world and human beings. He has the powers at his disposal which
first formed his own body, but which have then become increasingly

available for the activity of his 'I' once the astral and etheric forces have concluded their generative activities in the body. During the night, however, the human soul reimmerses itself completely in the spiritual music which it used at an earlier stage — in the embryonic period and during childhood — to construct the body. In Chapter 12 we called it 'Abel music.'

> If it is true that the human soul goes through devachan
> between two incarnations, we may also say that during the
> night the soul revels and lives in the streaming element of
> music from which it is woven and which is its true home.
> The creative musician, then, transforms the rhythms,
> harmonies and melodies which are imprinted on his etheric
> body during the night into physical notes. Unconsciously the
> musician possesses the spiritual world as his model which
> he turns into physical sound. That is the mysterious
> connection between the music which sounds here on earth
> and hearing spiritual music during the night.[96]

Once again we approach a musical work with the question whether it can guide us more deeply into the generative forces which we are pursuing physiologically in the forces of the astral body in human beings. Music must sacrifice its existence as a clever feast for the ears enjoyed by dreamers, and be liberated from its electronic mummification, by revealing the secrets with which it has impregnated human beings from the cosmos.

Chopin composed his Étude Op. 10, No. 12 at the age of 21. In its whole dynamic and structure it is dominated by a single interval, the seventh. It is tempting to see it virtually as an 'experiment to demonstrate the forces of the seventh.' Like a fountain the musical momentum plunges into the depths in the C minor dominant seventh chord. But the latter is positioned such by Chopin that the seventh, the B, frames the chord at both ends.

Example 13.

From this brightly illuminated seventh the music rushes *allegro con fuoco* into the sphere which Chopin places in opposition to the power of the seventh. The concentrated beam of seventh forces is directed at the firmest of the twelve keys: C minor. C minor binds together musically what in the context of the world is 'mineral solidification.' The latter is also the reason why Beethoven preferred this key. He sought it out when his willpower went in search of the hardest resistance; he created his works of art in the process of overcoming that resistance. But while with Beethoven everything happens within the equilibrium created by the polarities of the whole human being, Chopin takes it further to the extent that he often drives the musical elements into extremes of one-sidedness.

The C minor of the contra-octave bubbles up into the minor octave: its breathless motion which knows no break, only exhaustion towards the end, gains its shattering, churned up effect through the power of the seventh which brings the dead mineral element to life. We experience in musical terms how the life ether — otherwise far removed from consciousness — works in human beings.

A motif in the right hand supplies the support for this torrent of life:

Example 14.

In the middle of the piece (from bar 41), the repeat of the first part begins. But now the form-giving motif reveals the traces which the life ether process has left behind in it: it shows clear signs of the dissolution of the rhythmical and melodic framework (Example 15).

Example 15.

We experience artistically the transition into a pathological state. Immediately thereafter the strict harmony breaks up: there is an abrupt fall into D flat major followed immediately by F flat major (bars 65 and 67). The piece ends in C major; inwardly alive, radiating chords whose 'funereal character' (see above) appears to have been shed because the driving beat over 82 bars continues inwardly for the listener into the final four closing chords.

20.7 The chemical structure of parathormone

With the preceding steps we entered musically the life ether activity of the parathyroid glands. From a number of perspectives this physiological activity coincided with the musical quality of the seventh. On the basis of these musical patterns we will now attempt to understand the activity of the chemical ether which creates the physical carrier of the life ether, parathormone (hormone of the parathyroid glands). The following spiritual scientific context makes the next step possible:

> Just as we place images, Imaginations, before the soul, so on still higher levels the inner power of numbers is placed before human beings. Human beings have to learn to experience the inner proportions of numbers as spiritual music. Of particular importance, however, is the proportion 1:3:7:12. If you understand the proportion of these numbers as a musical relationship in the sense that one note oscillates three times in a given period, another seven, and still another one twelve, then you will find expressed in these numbers the relationship in spiritual music of the 'I,' astral body, etheric body and physical body.[97]

With the reference here to 'spiritual music,' it is clear once again that our physical music is a kind of reflection of the former. The value of such images is that they provide access to the archetypes.

The parathyoroid glands act as mediators between the dead calcium and the vital processes. They only appear in evolution at the point when animals come into direct contact with the earth; only land-based vertebrates possess parathyroid glands.[98] The physical body, which was given the number 12 in the above passage, is not identical with the mineral realm, but in the present phase of earth and human development it is filled with mineral matter. The activity of the life ether is the precondition for the activity of all the other etheric states in the human physical body. The physical and mineral body only maintains its link with the etheric body through the life ether. Thus, on the basis of our findings so far, we can put forward the hypothesis that the two numbers 7 and 12 will play a decisive role in the activity of the numbers ether (chemical ether or sound ether), which synthesizes parathormone in the parathyroid glands. For the relationship between the etheric body and the physical body is expressed in the proportion 7:12.

Parathormone is a polypeptide (protein molecule). Every protein consists of a series of amino acids. The various proteins are distinguished chemically by the type, number and sequence of these amino acids. The number of amino acids in parathormone was discovered in 1970 by Brewer and Niall independently of one another. Accordingly, parathormone consists of 84 amino acids.[99] The number 84 is also the product of 7 and 12.

In the above-mentioned Chopin Étude the life ether's activity metamorphoses into the structure of this work of art with such perfection that the piece has exactly 84 bars!

Such sound patterns are stages in the process which seeks to understand the activity of the astral body in the etheric types down to the level where physical matter is generated. Natural science and cognition through art coincide even where details are concerned. The molecules are returned into the wider setting of the whole human being, where they originated.

The extent to which musical laws and qualities provide insight into the physiological processes in human beings may seem surprising. But music takes a special place among all the arts as far as its link with the nature of human beings is concerned. We recall what Rudolf Steiner said in connection with a lecture by Walter Blume on music and the human being:

> The application of the findings of the science of the spirit to music in this way cannot be faulted. Nevertheless, care should be taken in applying this kind of observation to other arts in exactly the same way. It is possible with music precisely because the inner proportions of the 'I' are reflected exactly as unconscious proportions in the astral sphere. With painting, for example, one of the elements of the astral body falls out of the astral sphere in that mirroring process and into the physical body. ... So it is important that such a direct use of the constitution of the 'I' is only possible in music. This is what is particularly characteristic of the 'art of inwardness.'[100]

PART III

Respiratory Motion as Sculptural and Musical Archetype

The two sculptural exercises and the qualities of the intervals were the tools which we used in Parts One and Two to investigate various vital processes externally in the limbs and internally in organic processes. The etheric body which is active, on the one hand in the physical external world, and which on the other hand undergoes invagination inwardly into the soul sphere, liberating itself completely from the physical body in thinking activity — this duality was illustrated in Rudolf Steiners exercises.

In Part Three we will investigate respiration itself as mediator between these two processes together with the heart. In Part Four we will then move on to the external manifestation of heart and lung activity through the movements of music eurythmy.

21. The sculptural exercise for the etheric body of the lung

We have already noted above (see page 37), in the sculptural and musical representation of respiration between expansion and invagination, how closely the lung has remained connected with the impulses which underlie the human form as a whole. Respiration always retains those formative impulses like a homeopathic dose. The sculptural exercise which Rudolf Steiner suggested for the etheric body of the

Figure 37. (Daniel Moreau)

lung thus combines the two opposing principles of the first and the
second exercise. Whereas with the limb exercise the centre of the
sphere remains untouched, it is taken hold of and transformed in the
internal space exercise. The lung exercise combines both, as Rudolf
Steiner explained to the young doctors:

> Now, if you want to understand the three-dimensional
> human being, you also have to encompass the extremities. I
> can picture a sphere like this. I imagine that the sphere is
> stretched on the one side and infolded on the other. But now
> imagine that you go further and continue with the infolding

until you go beyond the bulge, then you will have this kind
of form, in fact two forms.

We are familiar with the first two steps (see Figure 38).

They are followed once again by invagination; but the question here
is, first, from which side and, second, in what way — as a single
indentation or like a fork (as in the limb exercise)?

Because the result is 'in fact two forms' it is clear that the fork-
shaped invagination is the one; but not on the side of the bulge but at
the rounded pole of the egg shape ('extended on the one side, infolded
on the other'), see Figure 39.

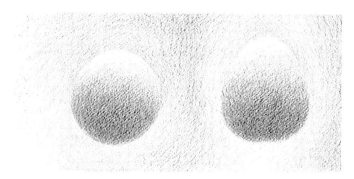

Figure 38.

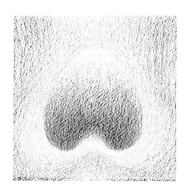

Figure 39.

We see the basic shape of the thorax. An archetypal form of the central sphere of the human being and thus of the whole human being has been created, to which we will return later when we examine the thorax. The breakthrough occurs when the first two exercises are combined, leading to a division. One shape turns into two.

Rudolf Steiner continues:

> But take this one step further so that these forms are not
> active only on the one side. Imagine that you do extension,
> invagination — extension, invagination; then an extra
> infolding from below and extension above and the result
> will be, if you do this three times, the sculptural form of the
> two lobes of the lung. In this way you will gradually begin
> to understand how the whole human being is linked
> inwardly with such forces.

It is not easy to understand what this means from the text version[101] we possess. What is clear, however, is that the two sections are meant to turn into the two lobes of the lung. Familiarity with the first two series of sculptural forms leaves little doubt that further invagination and extension is needed to produce these lobes together with ('from below') the invagination caused by the diaphragm as well as ('extension above') the apex of the lungs. 'If you do this three times' refers to the formation of the lobes — twice on the right side to produce the three segments and a further (third) time on the left to divide the lobe into two.

In this way the lungs are created from their proper tissue, the alveoli. The inversion exercise then produces the bronchial system with its continuation into the trachea and larynx, as we saw in the chapter on speech. We thus have to think of the etheric body of the lung as the combination of these two processes.

22. The etheric body as represented in the three exercises

The sculptural exercises for understanding the human etheric body show that the four constituent elements of the human being interpenetrate one another in three ways.

In the third stage the astral body intervenes and combines with the etheric body in two ways. In the limb exercise the etheric body takes the upper hand over the astral body to some extent, so that the invagination process does not create real cavities and the plantlike character of the limbs arises. In the inversion exercise the astral body dominates the etheric body and drives it inward from three-dimensional space into the musical region of the soul. The archetypal organ which mediates between inner and outer life, the lung, is created from a series of forms which combine both processes. The limb exercise leads to the solidification of the centre forces in the head. The metabolic exercise consists of the penetration and inversion of these centre forces. (Chapter 12 demonstrated how these two processes affect one another in the brain and the cerebrospinal fluid.) In the

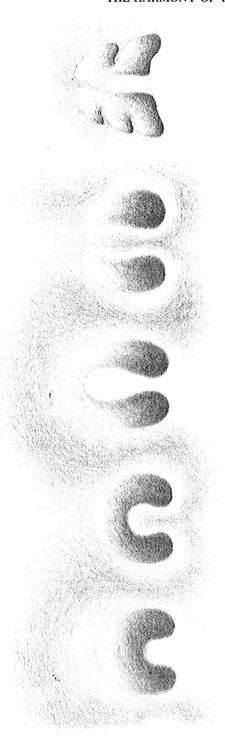

Figure 40.

lung's etheric body the saddle-like infolding process takes place as in the limb exercise; but at the same time the centre is penetrated as in the inversion exercise. The limb exercise leads to the image of the pentagram, the 'seal of the etheric body' (Steiner[102]), into which the external human form grows in five steps. The inversion exercise leads to the image of the self-devouring, self-sacrificing serpent in which the light of thinking shines. Thus the will and thought poles of the etheric body appears in two Imaginative symbols. The feeling, in contrast, reveals itself as the actual sphere of human incarnation to the extent that every physical organ assumes its physical form according to the archetypal image of respiration from the interaction of these two poles.

The connection with the physiology of the blood becomes directly apparent: the externally oriented side of the etheric body lives in the arterial blood whereas the more internally oriented side lives in the venous blood. Respiration acts between the two.

The lung is thus the organ which is closest to the sculptural archetype inhabited by the etheric body. That lies in its character as 'middle organ' which unites the extremes within itself. It is the same 'middle stage' at which the respiratory organ of plants, the leaf, revealed itself to Goethe in its archetypal nature. And he attempted to transfer this principle to the investigation of the human being; he was fully convinced that a general archetype based on the principle of metamorphosis was present in all organic creatures, could be observed in all its parts at certain middle stages and was to be recognized even where it withdrew modestly into concealment at the highest level, in mankind.[103]

This special position of the lungs is also raised by Rudolf Steiner in the course for young doctors:

> The lung is indeed formed by the respiratory forces, but so are the other organs. The difference is that it happens with the other organs in more or less roundabout ways whereas the lung is formed directly.

Then Steiner points out that this generative activity is only possible through a 'musical conception of its processes.'[104] In Part One we used the limb exercise to describe the power of respiration to create and form human beings, helping us to understand the musical and sculptural respiratory awareness of human beings in the Lemurian age,

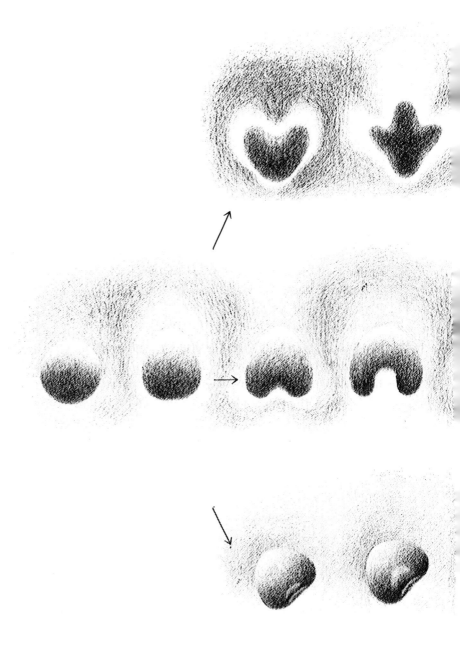

Figure 41. Three sculptural exercises as a whole. (Daniel Moreau)

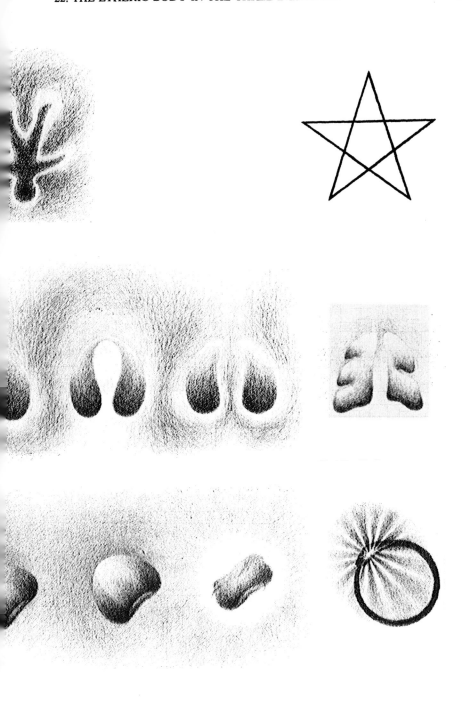

Figure 42. Ptah, the cosmic creator, forms the primal egg of life.

in which they experienced the creation of their organs in a dreamlike pictorial consciousness.

On the basis of the sculptural forms, the archetype of this early Lemurian human being would have to be associated with the egg shape. Rudolf Steiner's reading of the Akasha Chronicle confirms that: the human shape before the division of the sexes in early Lemurian times is formed in a way 'which can be compared with breaking out of an egg shape and the shedding of an egg shell.' 'For brevity's sake' Rudolf Steiner refers to the human ancestor from that stage of development as 'the egg human being.'[105] This evolutionary link is also the justification for inserting the egg shape into the inversion exercise. Rudolf Steiner acted accordingly in the lung exercise. (see page 130).

This gives us an inkling of what Figure 42 in the Egyptian mysteries was meant to illustrate. It represents the god Ptah sculpting the 'egg of life.'

> The cosmic egg from which all life originates is the central motif of a great many cosmogonies ... It is the 'egg of the waters,' the primal flood, the Nun. The chaotic primal waters initially underwent eightfold division, then created

the primal egg from which the sun god was born through
the 'eightfold divisions.'[106]

Thus the same Imaginative images occur in the language of egypto-
logists as we have discovered in the language of the modern mysteries
about the nature of the etheric. A thorough comparison between both
(see *Egyptian Myths and Mysteries* by Rudolf Steiner) would be an
important objective for the sculptural and musical study of organs.

23. The division of the etheric body into the sexes and the power of thinking

In the third stage of the plastic exercises two possibilities for infolding
arise. Here the hitherto unitary development divides. The one direction
leads outwards into the limbs. The other inwards into the processes
which are connected with the thinking in the etheric body. The two
exercises thus reflect in the etheric the will pole and the thinking pole.
In the etheric body of the lung we find the harmonious balance of
both processes, the basis for feeling.

In the third stage of earth evolution, in the 'Lemurian age,' this
division of the etheric and physical body into a form more closely
connected with the thinking and another form related to will development occurred in human evolution: the division into a male and a
female body which we have already touched upon in the context of
Chapter 13, 'Reproduction and thinking.'

It thus becomes clear in a different way how embryonic development and thinking development are connected in the etheric body and
why the history of ideas (see Chapter 14 'Development of organic
science') is essentially tied to male personalities. Men have the female
part of their etheric bodies available for inversion into the development of ideas because this part does not incarnate fully physically. In
this light the history of philosophy is 'written by men' only on a
physical level. A perspective which encompasses the world of the
etheric has to say that philosophy itself contains female human

influences in the form of thinking. In musical physiology this inversion takes place in the octave process of the head. This process, which is active in the physiology of the cerebrospinal fluid, is the image of the inversion by which the head is formed before birth from the body of the previous earth life. If we now take into account that the human being in the breathing process of his incarnations alternately incarnates as a man and a woman, this means that the results of the previous life which are contained in the head come, as a rule, from a physical body which had the opposite sex to the present one. The head of a man originates as a rule from an earlier female incarnation. The head of a woman originates as a rule from her previous male incarnation. Thus thinking must be seen as the activity of the male-female dual character of the soul which as it breathes uses the flow of the cerebrospinal fluid to fertilize its present life with the forces of its past life and its past life with the forces of its present life. And we can understand how the researcher of the spirit sees on an Imaginative level the same basic forms in the observation of thinking activity as natural science sees physically in embryonic development.[107] In this way the thinking is understood as the manifestation of a reincarnating being.

24. The structure of the thorax

24.1 The development of respiration in the lung

In the human skeleton the self-contained head with its spherical outer skeleton and the outwardly radiating limbs with the skeleton inside form two opposites. Such polarized forms are always the late result of a long development. In earlier stages of organic development there is still unity where later extreme polarization appears.

In its upper part the thorax is closed off in a headlike fashion; downwards, it opens up and displays in the final two free pairs of ribs distinct limblike characteristics. Thus the thorax shows in a single

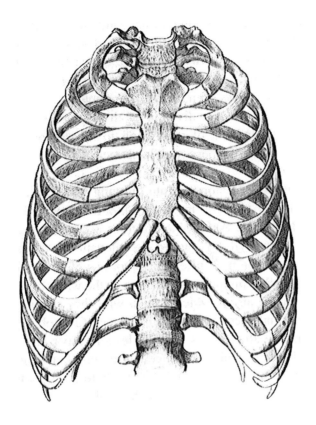

Figure 43. The rib-cage.

organ and in a balanced way what reaches extreme differentiation in the head and the limbs. As a consequence we have to understand the thorax as a creation preceding the head and the limbs. The simple rhythmical construction (metameric) of the early vertebrates is preserved here. In this sense a fish is 'pure thorax,' wholly a ribcage-entity. But at the same time it is also 'pure limb': its whole body becomes a limb when it propels itself along (the fins only serving for delicate manoeuvring). But it is also 'wholly head' in so far as a vital sensory organ characteristic of fishes, the lateral line system which detects pressure changes and vibrations, is not concentrated only in the head but is generally distributed over the whole body. Fishes represent organisms in which the archetype is still much more clearly physically apparent than in land-based animals. The archetype as the conceptual form of the etheric body is at home in the fluid element; it can therefore make itself physically apparent to a high degree. The step on to land leads to separation into two polarities: upwards into air on the one hand, in which the water has been rarefied into gas, and into earth on the other, in which it has been densified downwards. The step from water on to land leads to the division of the unitary structure into three parts. With the advent of respiration in the gaseous state the threefold structure is born whose middle element remains close to the original archetype.

The organ which is transformed into the lung is the air bladder. It is corrugated all over whereby ingrowing blood vessels gain contact with its internal cavities. An airpipe provides access to external air. (Detailed explanations will be found in the relevant text books. A fish thrown on land does not only suffer from shortage of air. Its desperate movements are much more pronounced than in the water because they lack resistance in the air — which is also why they remain without success. Land animals need organs of resistance for mobility, limbs. The slithering of the amphibians and reptiles still represents the 'fish movement' of the torso which has encountered resistance against the ground. The step from water to land thus leads to the internalization of respiration and the externalization of the limbs.

Thus the structure of the whole form shows the same sculptural development as we are able to observe in the respiratory organ and the limbs. Here fish fins still have to count as 'embryonic' limbs since in fishes the basic limb function is still present in the whole body.

With amphibians this simple lung remains very inefficient so that respiration still takes place largely through the skin. The outer skin of amphibians is therefore still mucous membrane. We will return to this kind of respiration, which takes place on the surface of the body, from the perspective of the internal physiology of respiration in human beings.

Through our understanding of the sculptural exercises, we can observe in Figure 44 the effect of the astral body, as it takes on physical form in the transition from gill-breathing to lung-breathing and imposes its own generative principles in the process.

In birth, human beings undergo the transition 'from water to land.' For as long as the body of the child is united in its fluid surroundings

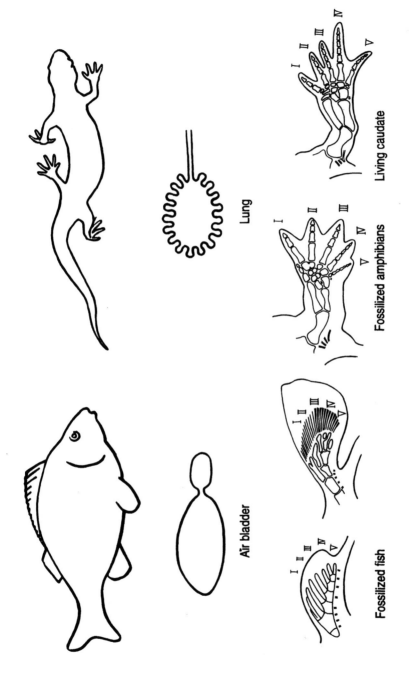

Lung

Living caudate

Fossilized amphibians

Air bladder

Fossilized fish

Figure 44. The step from water to land. Whole form, respiratory organ and limbs. The latter according to H. Steiner (1935) in: Starck, Vergleichende Anatomie, Vol.II, p.565).

with the maternal organism, the soul of the child is asleep in its environment, from which it awakes with the first breath. At one go the hitherto glandularly spongy lung is invaginated. Physical separation from the mother is the cause of this awakening and creates the precondition for the inner soul processes between mother and child which recreate on a higher level the link which has been physically severed.

Thus we can sum up the action of the astral body in the physical and etheric body in one sentence. We recall the intervention of the astral body in the third stage of the sculptural exercise (Figure 41), the division of the unitary structure of fish into three sections with the advent of pulmonary respiration in amphibians, and the first breath taken by the human being:

> The astral body *invaginates*
> and *divides,*
> in order to *awaken to feeling*
> in *moving* between the divisions.

If we look for the astral body in its own world, in music, this quality, which is mirrored in the physical and etheric body, is revealed there as the archetype of music, the interval. As we know, musical feeling is awakened in the movement between twó notes, which in themselves possess a physical and etheric character.

24.2 The sculptural anatomy of the thorax[108]

A closer look at the ribs in the upper part of the thorax, particularly the first pair, shows that they are curved edge-on. With the lowest ribs it is the surface which is curved. The ones in between show the various intermediate stages in that they start with surface curvature at the spine and rotate into edge-on curvature to a greater or lesser degree on their way to the sternum. The middle ribs are thus curved twice, once on the vertical axis and once on their own longitudinal axis.

If we sculpt the edge-on and surface curvatures, clearly defined variations in their quality can be experienced. The edge-on curvature might be characterized with the images 'bright, luminous and cool.' The surface curvature appears 'warm and somewhat dark.' We feel

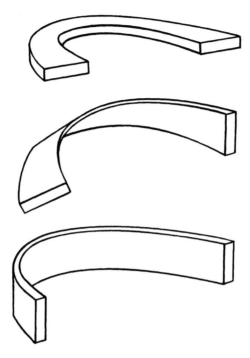

Figure 45. The first (top), the twelfth (bottom) and the middle ribs in diagrammatic form.

qualitatively what is expressed in technical and physical terms in the fact that the edge-on curvature places a great demand on the elasticity and plasticity of the material. With edge-on curvature the material is experienced as being subject to internal stress. In contrast, the surface curvature of a band involves much less inner materials stress. The doubly bent planes of the middle ribs have two axes of curvature around which the plane bends simultaneously. Every point of the doubly bent plane is thus involved in a movement going in two different directions simultaneously.

Point *P* simultaneously turns round axis *a* with movement *A* and round axis *b* with movement *B*. The physically visible plane is the resultant of two superimposed movements. As a consequence our experience of the plane loses the unambiguity which it has when the surface is curved in a simple convex or concave shape. It moves within itself and thus becomes alive.

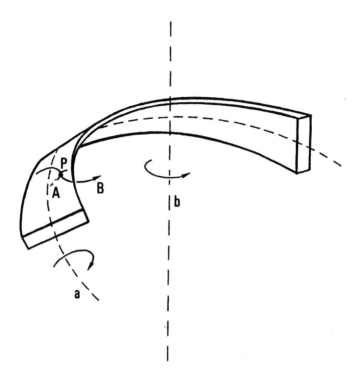

Figure 46.

That is why Rudolf Steiner told sculptors that the plane with its dual curvature was 'the simplest archetype of the inner life,' but also the way in which a plastic surface could be made 'to talk.'[109] But these two characterizations contain the essence of respiration in so far as it oscillates between inner stimulation and speech, between inhaling and exhaling.

In the thorax we found the archetype of the human skeleton brought a whole step nearer to physical manifestation than in the head and the limbs. Accordingly, the ribs are the original and most simple forms of the limbs. In human beings we should therefore observe that in early embryonic stages the arms and legs are closer in their form to the archetype of the ribs.

If we look at an embryonic stage at which the position of the arms and legs is still determined by their growth rather than by free movement, we see the following picture:

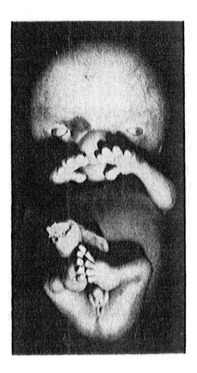

Figure 47. Embryo, eighth to ninth week. (From: Grosser, Ortman, Grundriß).

Once again we find confirmed that the astral body can make its archetype physically manifest to a much greater degree in water than 'on land': the arms demonstrate the developmental form of the upper ribs and the legs that of the lower ones. Whereas in later months the arms achieve free movement between pronation and supination, the tendency of the legs towards supination, which can be seen in the picture, remains until birth. Such findings prove that the archetype as we have described it is indeed the creative idea active in the organism. Otherwise the edge-on curvature of the arms and the surface curvature of the legs could not have been predicted from it.

24.3 The musical structure of the thorax

Anatomists have always distinguished between the so-called 'false ribs' and 'true ribs' in the thorax. The latter are given that name because they are connected directly to the sternum. The former do not reach the sternum but are connected to the ribs above or end freely like the two bottom pairs. The twelve pairs of ribs can thus be grouped into seven pairs of 'true ribs,' which form that part of the thorax oriented towards the head, and five pairs of 'false ribs' added below, which form the opening of the thorax as they become shorter (compare Figure 43).

It is tempting to interpret the division of the twelve pairs of ribs into groups of seven and five in the light of the various statements by Rudolf Steiner in which the relationship between these two numbers crops up. Formally, that would be using the numbers like an 'archetype' and the completely separate facts as its 'metamorphoses.' But that is dishonest if the connection between the facts and the numbers is not justified by their content. It is therefore our intention, before relating two different levels of perception to one another, to grasp these perceptions in their own living context. Once we have achieved a living understanding of the two different fields of observation, then a comparison will show whether we are dealing with metamorphoses of a joint archetype. Let us state here once and for all: an analogy is justified in its content when the two related facts can be presented convincingly as metamorphoses of the same archetype. We will thus begin by seeing whether the skeleton itself leads to a living concept of the division of the ribs into groups of seven and five.

The twelve ribs start at the spine. It, in turn, consists of twenty-four flexible vertebrae. The twelve thoracic vertebrae articulate with the twelve pairs of ribs. The remaining twelve vertebrae are divided into seven cervical and five lumbar ones. (The coccyx corresponds to the occipital bone; both consist of vertebrae which have fused and are no longer part of the spine.)

We can thus see from the skeleton itself that the astral body clearly works with the sevenfold division towards the head while the fivefold division is at work as we approach the metabolic pole. When this is

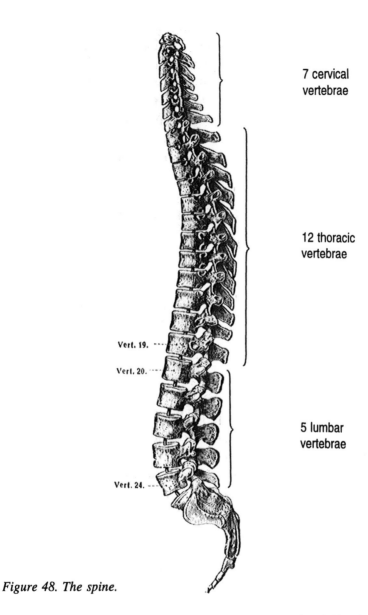

7 cervical
vertebrae

12 thoracic
vertebrae

Vert. 19.

Vert. 20.

5 lumbar
vertebrae

Vert. 24.

Figure 48. The spine.

linked with the sculptural perspective, we see the following: in the seven the organism closes itself off upwards; in the five it opens up downwards. These numbers in the arrangement of adjacent parts of the skeleton indicate the presence of the astral formative principle which operates on a higher level than the plastic one.

If we assume that the same generative forces can be observed in music as are active in the embryonic development of the body, we first of all have to look for a musical structure which reveals the same laws. Then we have to examine in this musical division whether we can observe with unbiased artistic feeling the same qualities which appeared in our observation of anatomical functions and in the living sculptural concept. Only then have we avoided an arbitrary numbers analogy and have observed musically the astral force which we have to conceive as being active in the etheric body.

There are twelve chromatic notes in our conventional tonal system. Seven of them form the diatonic scale. The remaining five produce a pentatonic scale.

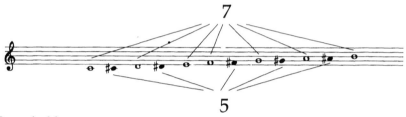

Example 16.

The artistic observation of the qualities which these two tonal systems possess will show whether their numbers can be related in substance to the point at issue.*

To begin with, let us feel the effect of a lullaby from the Hopi Indians.

Example 17.

---

* Maria Schüppel was the first to place this division of the chromatic 12-tone scale in the context of Gisbert Husemann's anatomical work on the ribs. (Working Week for the Study of the Human Being through Art 1975, Stuttgart.)

The following lullaby from Mongolia[110] has more earthlike solidity in that it is set within a bar structure:

Example 18.

If, finally, we still add a Gregorian chant from central Europe, we will have heard what Rudolf Steiner described as the 'mood of the fifth' from a number of different periods and parts of the world:

Example 19.

After these impressions, let us experience a classical diatonic song, Mozart's 'Komm lieber Mai und mache ...'[111]

Example 20.

or the Advent song 'Vom Himmel hoch, da komm ich her.'

Example 21.

A comparison of the qualities of these two moods allows us to characterize them as follows:

Pentatonic mood (five notes)	*Diatonic mood* (seven notes)
softness	contoured (through semi-tones, cadences)
openness (fourth and octave experience are missing)	Self-contained through fourth and octave experience
floating, flowing, dreamlike	tonic-oriented, stationary, awake

We need not pursue the comparison further here. After all, in a book we can only refer to musical experiences which, to a greater or lesser degree, must be assumed in the reader.

Let us now return with these two musical qualities to the thorax. There we find the number seven where the organism closes itself off, and the number five where it opens. In functional terms of the upper human being, we find the greater wakefulness in the region of the seven. The five is connected with the dreamlike, sleeping consciousness of the metabolic organs. If we recall that the five lower pairs of ribs essentially no longer enclose the lungs, but the blood organs liver, spleen and kidneys, we encounter once again the ceaselessly flowing life of the pentatonic mood on an organically functional level.

The correspondences which we have found as a result of our observation of the soul lead to the conclusion that the diatonic system reflects an activity of the astral body whose cosmic creative archetype was also active in the development of the upper thorax. In the pentatonic mood we experience the generative activity with which the astral body resounds in the etheric body in the lower thorax. This musical body is at work in the nervous system with the 'seven' and in the blood with the 'five.'

25. The image of the middle human being

In their middle, rhythmical organs, human beings provide the balance for what exists in opposition in the nervous and sensory system and the metabolic and limb system. Placed between the thinking and imagination in the head and the will activity of the feet and hands, feeling has its physiological base in the lungs and the heart. Relating soul processes to parts of the organism in this way simply indicates the organs where the soul functions are based. The thinking lives in the whole human being but is concentrated especially in the cerebral region. Feeling lives in the whole human being, but particularly in the middle respiratory zone. The will lives in the whole human being, but particularly in the limbs.

How do heart and lungs fit into this polarity? Through the separation of the cerebrospinal fluid, the solidity of the brain opens itself to participation in the life of the middle human being, for the latter lives in the flow of blood and air. The involvement of the cerebrospinal fluid in the respiratory rhythm can be observed if in the aspiration of the vertebral canal a manometer is attached to the needle. The column of liquid rises with inhalation and falls with exhalation.

That is easily confirmed if one puts one's hand on the anterior fontanelle of an infant; one can then observe how it rises as the child breathes in and falls as it breathes out. It is, then, in the first instance the rhythm of the lungs which continues into the cerebral region, rather than that of the heart.

The heart shows its connection with the limbs in that it is muscle throughout. The lung represents the conscious upper human being in the middle sphere: breathing can be controlled voluntarily and serves the thinking through language. The heart, a muscle involuntary in its action, is more distanced from the consciousness. A person is healthy if the lungs and the heart can balance this polarity. In that case the two extremes which are present in human beings are prevented from coming to expression in a pathological manner. If the rhythmical system fails, one of these two extremes dominates the whole. That can extend as far as the external shape of the body so that the whole person is taken hold of by the formative principle of the lower or the upper human being. The two patients depicted below are an example of this.

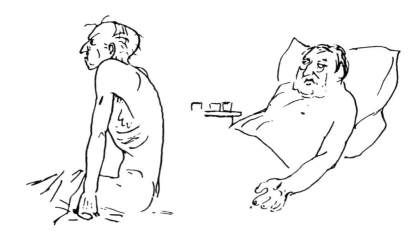

Figure 49. Dyspnoeic-cachectic type A of severe chronic bronchitis, 'Pink Puffer' (left); and cardialgic-hypoxic type B of severe chronic bronchitis, 'Blue Bloater' (right). (From Brewis, in Gross, Schölmerich, Lehrbuch).

Both patients are suffering from severe chronic bronchitis. The inflamed mucous congestion of the respiratory tracts leads first to the restriction of the airflow and finally to the degeneration of lung tissue and emphysema. The main symptom of this illness is the shortage of breath. Now the patient on the left reacts in quite a different way to this than the one on the right. The left patient breaths more deeply and rapidly. With great mental and physical effort he fights for air. The physical labour of trying to breathe leads him to lose weight until he reaches the stage of cachexia.* This patient develops pronounced emphysema with the corresponding rigid and enlarged chest. The patient on the right does not even notice that his illness is connected with shortage of breath. He feels hardly any difficulty in breathing. And the way in which he seeks to compensate for the shortage of breath takes placed under the threshold of consciousness. He does not increase his breathing but forms more blood (secondary polycythaemia). The blood

* Greek: *kaks,* bad; *héxis.* condition. Cachexia: emaciation.

can fix more oxygen because more red blood cells flow into the lung
— the blood becomes thicker. This patient only has reduced emphysema. He suffers from heart insufficiency and has a tendency to
obesity. Various degrees of seriousness can be found between these
two extreme forms of chronic bronchitis.

If we observe this from the perspective of the threefold structure of
the human being we can see that in the absence of the middle system
the emaciated patient comes too much under the influence of the
sensory and nervous forces: he experiences consciously the cause of
his illness and reacts with that upper part of the middle system which
is nearer to consciousness, the lungs. The same illness causes the fat
patient to sink into the heaviness of the metabolic forces. He is
'asleep,' both as regards his illness itself and in the way that he deals
with it. Blood formation in the bone marrow is still further removed
from consciousness than even the digestion.

We can take both images further with the following thought: the
different human illnesses are embodied around us in the various
animal types. Malformation of the feet from an orthopaedic point of
view, for instance, can be found in various animal species in a healthy
and appropriate form.[112] With this in mind, we can ask in relation to
the two patients which animal form best represents the tendency of the
thin patient fighting for breath. If we observe the way in which he
reacts to the illness from his head, how he lives in greatly intensified
respiratory motion, wide awake and with his expanded, rigid chest,
while withdrawing from the gravitational forces of the metabolism
(emaciation), we can recognize a birdlike character. We can take the
eagle as representative for the birds in the way that they physically
overcome the air. Alongside the birdlike character we have belladonna
as the medicine for this patient, a plant which embodies this birdlike
development in a similar way.[113]

The animal form which is completely given over to metabolic
processes, to gravity, so that digestion takes place in several stomachs
and through rumination, is the cow. What is healthy in the cow
overwhelms the other patient, who has a tendency towards obesity,
whose blood level is rising and who is less awake overall. Thus we
can see the opposites, between which the rhythmical system has to
maintain equilibrium, in the image of the eagle and the cow. Both

are active as cosmic forces in the upper and lower human being, as we find stated in Rudolf Steiner's lectures of October 1923.[114] There we also find a description of the Imagination of the rhythmical system:

> With the lion it is the case that there is a kind of
> equilibrium between respiration and blood circulation ... The
> cerebral qualities are developed in the lion such that
> respiration is balanced by the rhythm of the circulation.

Thus we have the lion as the image of the middle human being between the eagle and the cow. With wakeful attention, the gaze of the lion transmits the warmth in which the eye of the cow is lost in sleep and from which the eagle's gaze has released itself in over-wakefulness into the pure luminous atmosphere.[115]

Within the animal world the cow and the eagle in turn appear closer to human beings than for example the whale and the lark.

25.1 The path from sculptural to musical structures

Having taken the step from sculpture to music several times and in a variety of ways, we will insert here some concluding methodological remarks.

Rudolf Steiner showed a number of paths from sculptural to musical structures of which we have already encountered a few.

The experience of specific motion from the inside to the outside or vice versa, such as in the blood circulation and respiration, corresponds equally to the spiritual scientific description of major and minor and to our direct musical experience. Such a path can be followed with each of the numerous musical qualities which Steiner interpreted physiologically (in the music eurythmy lectures). We pursued this line above all in Part Two, which dealt primarily with internal physiological processes. Thus every musical quality (intervals, rhythm, harmony, etc.) can, as such, be compared with the living image of an organic process. The classic picture in Rudolf Steiner is the relationship between foot and head activity as the relationship between the prime and the octave. In working with Rudolf Steiner's notes, one has to be aware that he did not make a distinction in the way he expressed himself between steps and intervals. Indeed, a step can also be understood as the functional expression of an interval within the scale. In line with Steiner, we use the terms for the intervals in the sense of their functional value as steps.

The second path goes via numbers. As we explained above, the sound or numbers ether arises in the development of the etheric body through the intervention of the astral body. That is the origin of the mathematical structure of organisms which we encountered in the proportions of growth and, most recently, in the thorax and the spine. Rudolf Steiner's work on the physiology of the lung follows this path and will be dealt with below. He shows how the fifth in the lung is reached through the proportion 2:3 (see page 163).

> The astral body enumerates the etheric body, but in doing so it differentiates. It forms the etheric body through enumeration. Between the astral body and the etheric body we find numbers, and they are something living which is alive and active in us.[116]

> Just as we place images, Imaginations before the soul, so in a certain sense we place the inner force of numbers before the human being on a still higher level, and he has to learn to experience the inner relationships of numbers like spiritual music.[117]

The step from sculpture (anatomy and physiology) to music takes place here in the sense that Goethe summed up his method:[118]

1. The enumeration of elements in existing anatomical and physiological phenomena: the empirical phenomenon.
2. The establishment of mathematical proportions in accordance with anatomical and physiological relationships and experiments with the monochord. These experiments can express the inner nature of the mathematical proportions as the relationship between two different notes: the scientific phenomenon.
3. The application of musical appreciation to these two notes. This reveals the inner quality they possess as an interval. We understand the generative soul force (astrality) which is hidden in the empirical phenomenon: the pure phenomenon.

Another point of access is music eurythmy. That will be discussed in Part Four.

Finally, it is particularly satisfying if a sculptural and musical relationship in the organism returns in a musical work of art through the metamorphosis of the generative forces.

The focus of musical consciousness onto the sculptural activity of organs trains the thinking for Inspiration, which thereby gains life as the will in embryonic form. Using an image of Inspiration, Rudolf Steiner compares the soul forces used for natural science with the soul forces used for higher knowledge: the higher cognitive forces have the same relationship to the ordinary ones as the musical ear does to perception which is only directed at the vibrating string of the instrument (Steiner[119]).

26. The sound of the middle human being

26.1 The thorax as the sphere of the 'objective intervals'

The sculptural form of the ribs and their musical structure reflect in the upper thorax the consciousness-waking, antipathetic effect of the generative forces, and in the lower thorax their soporific, sympathetic action. What we see in sculptural terms in the thorax originates essentially in time, in the rhythm of waking and sleeping. This rhythm, too, is clearly involved in the development of the thorax; a vital rhythm in which respiration in the lung becomes part of a transcending order. If we now look for the physical movement which is linked with the sleeping-waking rhythm as intimately as respiration is linked with thoracic and pulmonary motion, this movement will not be found in the human organism. On the contrary, it is a motion which the human body has in common with the earth, namely the rotation of the earth around its own axis. The latter is the 'time clock' for the twenty-four-hour rhythm of sleeping and waking. During these twenty-four hours, human beings experience once the totality of all the

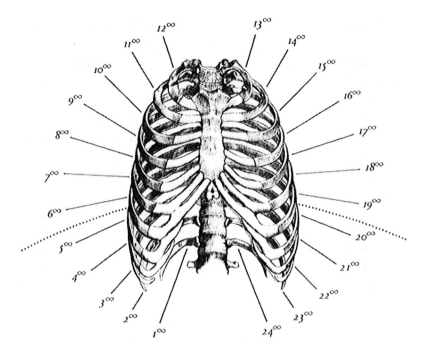

Figure 50.

stars as represented in the twelve signs of the zodiac. Let us return from this image to the thorax. Twelve different ribs are duplicated symmetrically to form a 'cage' of twenty-four ribs. In the sculptural, musical and linguistic image of the thorax which we have developed, the latter reflects spatially in the polarity of its ribs and its mathematical order the temporal form of waking and sleeping. Let us assume this as a hypothesis for the time being.

The rhythm of sleeping and waking is in turn embedded in the rhythm of spiritual life between death and birth and physical life between birth and death. This rhythm, too, is reflected in the construction of the thorax. Rudolf Steiner describes the speed with which the soul rises in the spiritual world until it reaches the turning point of the 'cosmic midnight hour,' and the speed with which it descends into a new incarnation, as being reflected in the proportions between the upper part of the torso (thorax) and the lower part (abdomen).

> If this part from the middle of the chest to the neck is
> shorter than the lower part of the torso we are dealing with
> a person who in the time between death and birth had a
> spiritual life in which he rose very quickly to the midpoint.
> That went very fast. It was followed by slow and
> comfortable progress down to a new life on earth.[120]

Here too a temporal process (speed) is given three-dimensional form
in the thorax.

It is clear from the context that the region of the diaphragm should
be taken as the middle.

Below, we will show how the different proportions of thorax and
abdomen are also reflected in the sleep requirements of the body.
Rudolf Steiner links the construction of the body with the sleeping-
waking rhythm and with the reincarnation rhythm between spiritual
life and physical life. It is decisive from our point of view that the
physical representation of the cosmic midnight hour as middle sphere
between the abdomen and the thorax coincides with our representation
of physical midnight which we arrived at from quite a different angle.
It confirms our hypothesis (Figure 50). In a more specialist, spiritual
scientific explanation of the physiology of respiration, Rudolf Steiner
goes on to explain the origin of the ribs themselves. Although at the
start of embryonic development the head shoots ahead of everything

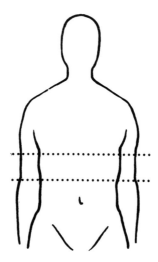

Figure 51.

else, the embryo later becomes subject to 'the forces which rhythmically circle the earth in parallel to its surface. The thorax is formed, and is in fact created from the currents which circulate around the earth. These currents are reproduced, if you like, in the ribs.'[121] Thus spiritual science confirmes the image of the thorax as reflection of the earth's rotation.

If we wanted to experience the musical link between the thorax and the etheric streams circulating the earth, it would mean developing a consciousness which mankind possessed in very early stages of its development. We have already mentioned this consciousness in connection with the creation of the human form through the respiratory activity which formed the body. Human beings in Lemurian times felt that they shaped their bodies through breathing in 'tonal images' in association with the gods. Before the descent of human beings from their surroundings onto earth, 'body' did not refer to one made of physical matter. The physical body was not yet filled with mineral but with etheric substance. The further we go back in history, the greater become the gaps between the notes which human beings felt to be musically 'useful' intervals. From modern history of music we know that it is only in the twentieth century that the second begins to mean more to musicians than merely a dissonance 'in need of resolution.' Before that the third had to be conquered. Earlier still, the fourth was a 'forbidden' interval which was felt to be dissonant. Accordingly, Rudolf Steiner describes how in still earlier times the scales themselves consisted of much larger intervals. In the Atlantean period music was experienced in scales of sevenths. In the period before human incarnation on earth (middle of the Lemurian age) human beings experienced music in scales of ninths in the same way that seconds are used as the steps of the scale today.

Thus a fifth comprised four ninths in that period:

Example 22.

People experienced music in quite a different way in that primeval time. The whole human being still possessed a purely etheric and astral bodily nature. Steeped in deep dream-consciousness, he did not experience music as something of his own but he felt the musical experience of the creative spiritual beings (hierarchies) in whose lap he lived. This musical experience of four thousand years ago now reveals a very curious relationship to the musical experience of our present fifth cultural epoch. Our feeling for major and minor represents a relatively recent phase of musical history which is already on the wane. Our early Lemurian ancestor also apparently experienced (jointly with the gods, however) a kind of major-minor tonality. This was lost to mankind with the descent to earth; it is out of the question in the Atlantean sevenths scales. Only after the events connected with Golgotha does it reappear in a more spiritual form with the age of Bach. In the earlier period a triad had an expansive, truly etheric sound through the steps of ninths which today we can, of course, only guess at from the indications given by Rudolf Steiner:

Example 23.   *Lemurian,*   *Contemporary,*
                     objective major mood   *subjective major mood*

What we described today as the inner experience of the
major mood was experienced by him, in being removed
from his body, as the cosmic celebratory singing, the cosmic
celebratory music of the gods, the expression of their joy
about their cosmic creation. And our inner experience today
of the minor mood was experienced for the first time by
human beings in the Lemurian age as the immense sorrow
of the gods at the possibility that human beings could
become prey to what is later described in the biblical story
as the fall from grace — the breaking away from the divine
spiritual powers, from the powers of goodness.[122]

If we set the fingering on the monochord for the objective fifth which we have described, the proportion of 24:1 appears:

Example 24.

The 'currents circulating the earth' leave the imprint of their musical generative forces in the temporal shape of the twenty-four hour period in the same way as they do in the twenty-four ribs of the thorax: both instances represent the incarnation of the objective fifth. As we saw, the rotation of the earth is the physical 'organic motion' of the sleeping-waking rhythm. We can thus see in the interval 24:1 the proportion which contains the relationship between the earth (= 1) and the thorax with its twenty-four sections. The Lemurian experience of music enables us to understand the cosmic relationship of the thorax to the earth. The relationship of the twenty-four ribs to the earth as a single entity is the correlation of the musical experience of human beings in Lemurian times, which was not tied internally to their bodies but which lived in the forces which united their bodies with the cosmos as a whole.

26.2 The lung

If we take a further step inwards, the lung is situated under the ribs. We repeat the step from the sculptural to the musical sphere with the lung and count two sections in the left lobe and three in the right one. We separate the string of the monochord into five parts. Then we divide it into 2/5 and 3/5. If we play both parts of the string the proportion 2:3 sounds, the fifth.

Example 25.

Here we find the justification for Rudolf Steiner's words: 'The relative proportions of the lobes of the lung will give you a fifth' (Steiner[123]). The fifth is thus present here too as the principle which underlies the shape of the lung. But it is the modern subjective fifth, to which we are accustomed. The beginning of Bruckner's Fourth Symphony can help to make its character clear. All of it is drawn from the world of the fifth.

Example 26.

The acceleration of the rising second fifth in the horns particularly reinforces the character of this interval. It makes the second B flat float as if it were 'on wings in an upcurrent.'

The fifth thus works in the construction of the middle human being from the perspective of two different worlds. It does so as objective cosmic fifth in the outer skeleton and as subjective earth fifth in the construction of the lungs. United, both sound as in Example 27.

Example 27.

Compared to the airlike quality of the subjective, contemporary fifth, the great, objective fifth is filled with radiant light.

A glance at the physiological relationship between the thorax and the lungs deepens this musically anatomical picture: in the lung the blood reaches the frontier with the outside world through a membrane in a similar fashion to the way that it gives us an experience of the fifth. We studied this in Part Two and heard it in the example of the Bruckner symphony. Rudolf Steiner makes a direct physiological connection between the fifth and the skin as the frontier of the body. In the lung it is the inner skin for the blood. Thus the external proportion 2:3, resulting from the way that the lungs are segmented, converges with the inner quality. The previously mentioned quality of the sixth leads to that activity of the lungs through which carbon dioxide penetrates the membrane and flows into the environment. The fifth lives in the blood which flows tangentially through the alveolar membrane. The sixth lives in the air process of gaseous exchange, if this is perceived as the internal equivalent of the activity of the feet as in Part Two.

As empty membrane, the lung does not have the strength to maintain its form. If it had to rely on its own powers, it would collapse (pneumothorax). It is held in shape through external forces, through the thorax. Neither can it move by its own power. It is moved by the muscles of the thorax and by the diaphragm. The inner wall of the thorax and the outer surface of the lung are respectively covered by a further membrane, the parietal and visceral pleura. Both membranes secrete fluid so that they are permanently moist. Reduced air pressure in the gap between the parietal and visceral pleura creates the suction which holds the lung from outside to the wall of the thorax. Thus the shape of the lung is preserved through suction by the thorax, and it moves through the lubricated surfaces of both organs sliding against one another tangentially. This allows us to see on a physiological level the image which is revealed musically in the 2:3 proportion of the lung's 'subjective fifth,' whose shape is preserved through suction by the forces of the cosmic objective fifth.

26.3 Respiration and lung metabolism

If we penetrate more deeply into the activity of the lung it becomes impossible to find fixed shapes. We encounter a mass of flowing air in the interior of the pulmonary tree which brushes past the most finely branched currents of blood. Here the blood is constantly transformed from its venous into its arterial quality. This transformation is the physiological site of the equilibrium of blood and respiratory activity which we have seen in our case studies. The carbon dioxide which is formed through the activity of the will evaporates from the blood into the gases of the lung; the oxygen from the environment is fixed by the blood from the inflowing air. If we seek to express this in a numerical equation, it can only be in terms of flowing quantities in time. Now modern physiology has an exact understanding of the relationship between blood and respiratory movement in the lungs. The 'ventilation-perfusion quotient' is referred to as an important quantity in the physiology of the lungs. The quantity of air per minute which interacts with the blood (ventilation volume) has a relationship with the quantity of blood per minute which interacts with the air (perfusion volume) of 4:5 in a healthy person. Only the ventilation volume itself is used for the calculation — in other words, only the air which is in direct contact with the blood. The 'dead space ventilation,' that is, those quantities of air which move in the bronchi without having contact with the blood, is subtracted. Proportionately, then, five litres of blood flow around four litres of air in a set period of time (Sill, et al.[124]).

The absolute values of perfusion and ventilation can of course vary greatly depending on the degree of strain. If we run fast and the blood circulation in the lungs increases, respiration is speeded up by the amount necessary to preserve the 4:5 relationship. Conversely, if less air enters and leaves a lobe or segment of the lungs due to the partial shift of a bronchus, then the blood circulation is selectively reduced in that section of lung to the necessary level to maintain the perfusion-ventilation relationship of 4:5 as far as the illness permits. It affects the lung also to the extent that it is probably the only internal organ which is directly affected by gravity in its blood circulation.[125] When a person is standing upright, the lower, basal parts of the lung have a higher blood circulation than its apex. If that person is lying on his back, the (dorsal) parts nearest the back have a higher blood circulation than those towards the front wall of the thorax. The blood in the lung submits to the gravity of the earth, represented in the forces of the cow, to the same extent that the lung as organ of the air withdraws — with its eagle forces — from the earth. In all these various zones, in which the blood circulation varies according to gravitational influence, the astral body regulates respiration in accordance with the relationship 4:5. (See Figure 52).

Figure 52. Representation of the blood circulation (Q) and ventilation (V) in various positions of the body and after physical labour (After Allgöwer).

The relationship between ventilation and perfusion is the decisive factor governing the oxygen and carbon dioxide content of the blood.[126] This quotient of respiratory and blood flow increases from the basal part of the lung to its apex from 0.63 to 3.3 in a person standing upright and at rest. Thus the apex of the lungs contains about five times as much air as blood.[127] The ventilation-perfusion quotient of 4:5 mentioned earlier applies to the lung as a whole.[128] The above differences only apply at rest, and balance themselves out with physical work.

If, now, we allow 4/9 and 5/9 of the string on the monochord to sound, we will hear the following interval as the relationship between these two notes:

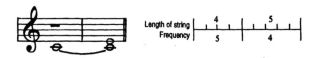

Example 28.

This major third, then, is the musical image of those astral forces which preserve the equilibrium between the blood and respiration. If we recall the fifth and its connection with the shape of the lung, the way in which it presents an empty structure suspended in air, the experience of the third brings us into inner contact with the warmth of the blood. The gaseous expansiveness of the fifth makes the transition to the inner warmth of the blood which flows from and returns to the heart.

With this we have understood a step which mankind took with the withdrawal of the soul from its surroundings:

> There was the experience of the fifth, in which human
> beings still felt connected with what lived in their
> respiration ... They felt ... that they were breathing in and
> breathing out ... but the musical experience was not part of
> them, it lived in their breathing in and breathing out. This
> experience of music made them feel as if they were leaving
> themselves and then returning. The fifth was something
> which grasped inhaling and exhaling ... The third made it
> possible for (modern) human beings to experience the
> internal continuation of the respiratory process (Steiner[129]).

This is possible because the respiratory process, in extending inwards, enters the 4:5 relationship with the blood in the way that has been shown by modern physiology.

This also explains how at birth the major third, as the developmental impulse of the astral, becomes evident in the proportions of the infant (compare Figure 30). With the first breath air and blood shoot into the lung. The other internal organs have already begun to function in the womb. Through birth they merely function more intensively and in different ways. The lungs, in contrast, have to begin functioning in one go. During the first months, the major third establishes the equilibrium between blood and air flow in the lung and from there in the whole body of the infant.

We dealt with the step from aqueous to land-based life near the beginning of this part in the context of the phylogenesis of organisms. We saw that the amphibians with their simple lungs breathe primarily through the skin. Air and blood thus come into contact very much on the outside, on the surface of the skin in amphibians. In sculptural terms, the organic process which later becomes invaginated internally still lives on the surface. Accordingly, the astral body too has been little internalized. In the archetype of the animal world, the human being, we found the proportion between blood and air to be 4:5. If we look at amphibians (Figure 44), however, we will see this proportion there too, except that it appears sculpturally on the outside in the respiration of the skin: they possess four toes on their front feet and five at the back. The astral body which is still wholly breathing on the outside, does not establish the air-blood proportion internally, but in external sculptural terms. The air process which is closer to conscious-ness is reflected logically in the front limbs through the number four; the processes of the blood which are further from consciousness are reflected in the back limbs in the number five. In accordance with its nature, the major third only comes to expression when it can manifest itself in internal respiration.

In recognizing the major third as the 'continuation of the respiratory process to the inside,' the physiology of respiration manifests itself in three different metamorphoses of the fifth which the human soul has undergone in the way it experiences music; that is, in the progress from the Lemurian age via the post-Atlantean Greek period to the present:

— as cosmic fifth in the external skeleton (formed with ninths);
— as physical, gaseous fifth in the shape of the lungs (formed with seconds);
— as internalized fifth in the major third, the force of equilibrium between air and blood. It can also be understood as being a 'chromatic fifth': five semitones form a major third (as pointed out by Maria Schüppel).

In moving from the outside to the inside of the organism, we can thus grasp through musical physiology the steps by which the human soul learns to feel its own nature in the rhythm of its development.

26.4 Lungs and heart

If, as step four, we now follow the blood which flows inwards from the lungs, we reach the heart. Whereas the blood in the lungs evaporates into the environment, it meets resistance in the heart. It is dammed up in itself.[130] At the same time the heart causes the blood flow to change direction. As it enters and leaves the heart, the blood flows through the heart valves. It flows in through five cusps — the sum of the cusps in the tricuspid and the mitral valves. It flows out past six cusps (the sum of the aortic and pulmonary valves).

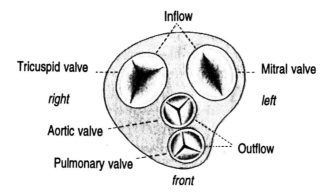

Figure 53. Schematic view of the heart valves from above (after removal of the vestibules).

It is between the inflow which moves five cusps and the outflow which moves six, that the change of direction takes place, the reversal from diastole to systole, the damming up of the blood in the apex of the heart. Transferred to the monochord, the change from 5:6 sounds as a minor third.[131]

Example 29.

The polarity which characterizes the blood as it flows between heart and lungs is summed up in the following Figure:

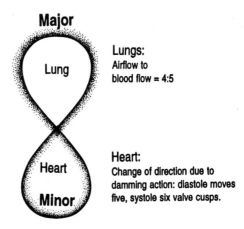

Figure 54.

When it reaches the pulmonary alveoli, the blood flows into a zone with the mighty surface area of approximately 70 m², which is only accommodated in the thorax because of its millionfold invaginations. The blood is transformed into an extremely fine film; it becomes membrane in the process of the fifth. Refreshed from the environment, it flows back into the heart where it is dammed up and comes to rest for 1/10 of a second. We already dealt with that in Part One. At that stage we defined the minor mood which characterizes the heart purely in terms of the dynamic of its movement. Here it is shown to exist in anatomical terms by the outer path of the numerical proportions.

The objection has been raised on occasion that it is inconsistent to make a comparison between the volume of blood and air which flows through the lungs, while counting valve cusps in the heart. But this objection fails to acknowledge that the character of the lung is quite different from that of the heart. From our perspective here the heart has the following physical characteristics: it interrupts the blood flow, it is an organ of densification which introduces death into the life of the blood so that the 'I' can awaken to consciousness in the blood. In this context the movement of physically fixed parts is important. A certain flexibility in thinking is required and it is wrong to try to understand the physical structures of two organs, which are diametrically opposed, as if they were identical.

There is a continuous struggle in the middle human being between the major and minor forces. In the lungs, the organ of the air, the astral body predominates. In the heart, the muscle, it is the etheric body. Here too we encounter the musical physiology of human beings in the spiritual scientific description of the major and minor mood:

> A kind of struggle ensues between the sentient body [astral body] and the etheric body. If these tones are so strong that they overcome the inherent tones of the etheric body, joyful music is created in the major key. If music is in the major key the astral body has prevailed over the etheric body. In the minor key the etheric body prevails over the astral body. The etheric body resists the oscillation of the astral body (Steiner[132]).

As our musical experience of the flowing motion encounters resistance in the fixed point of the heart, we have to understand the resultant

minor mood in the language of the 'I.' 'The etheric body resists the
oscillation of the astral body'; in sculptural terms we see the blood
flow striking against muscle.

As a consequence the complete sound of the middle human being is:

Example 30.

If this chord is played on stringed instruments the result is a self-
contained harmony which simultaneously radiates far through space.
It is almost as if one might become aware of the source of the permanent healing powers which emanate from these organs.

Let us recall once more our two case studies. The developmental
tendencies of the bird have taken hold of the patient whose lungs are
distended and who reacts to his shortage of breath through his
respiration. The developmental forces of the cow have seized hold of
the other person who reacts to his lung disease through his blood
production. The middle system in between is like the lion which
subdues the excessive force of the breathing while countering the
weight of gravity in the blood.

The step towards the inside from sculpture to music, from image to
sound, becomes a spiritual step towards the outside. It is the step from
the image which is the product of the sensory world to the inner
musical contact with the subtle reality of the spirit which underlies the
soul. It is a preliminary step, starting in the physical world, towards
the Inspirative understanding of the astral body.

Anyone who observes the external structure of the human
being, in so far as it is dependent on the astral body, has to

> study physiology, not as a physicist but as a musician. And
> he has to know the inner music which forms the human
> organism (Steiner[133]).

The music which we possess today can be a stage on the path to the
inwardly formative, spiritual music.

26.5 Asymmetry as a principle of the fifth

The dynamic of the fifth can be observed in the asymmetrical
embryonic development of the lungs. It will lead us from the 'sound
of the middle human being' to his 'word.'

In the three-week-old embryo, which measures about three
millimetres crown to rump, the site of development of the lungs
appears as a forward pointing invagination of the front wall of the
primitive gut. The lung bud divides after a further three weeks. The
right offshoot grows steeply downwards while the left one is somewhat retarded in its growth and develops horizontally to the left. A
little later the division of the lungs into three lobes on the right and
two on the left can be seen.

> At this stage of development [when the embryo is about
> five millimetres long] they already begin to become
> asymmetrical in that the right lung grows more rapidly in a
> vertical direction whereas the left lung lies more hori-
> zontally (Broman[134]).

How can this asymmetry be explained? The growth potential of
the three elements of the body not only varies by degree, but is also
polarized into extremes: the lack of regenerative power in the sensory
and nervous system stands in contrast to the reproductive vitality
in the lower metabolic and limb system which is strong enough for
the reproduction of the whole organism. The low vitality of the senses
and the brain rejects the etheric body which frees the latter from
its physical vital functions and allows its activity to metamorphose
into the production of perceptions and ideas. The high level of vitality
in the metabolic organs in the abdomen is accompanied by will
impulses which impinge only weakly on the consciousness. The
organs of the middle in the thorax oscillate rhythmically within this

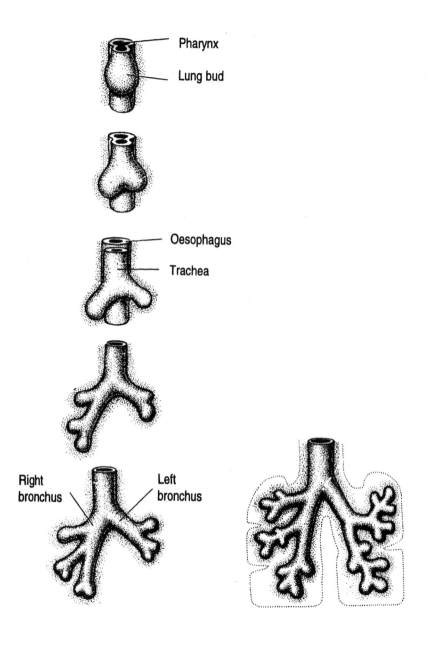

Figure 55. The development of the bronchial tree and the lungs during the first eight weeks of life of the embryo. (From: Moore, Embryologie).

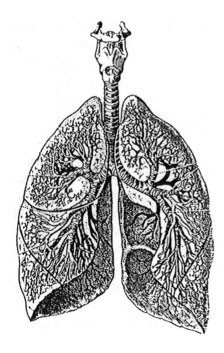

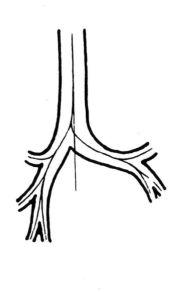

*Figure 56. Lungs and larynx
in the adult. (From: Benninghoff,
Lehrbuch).*

*Figure 57. The branching of the
trachea in a living person with the
longitudinal axes drawn in. (Braus).*

polarity — the lung closer to consciousness, the heart further removed from it.

If against this background we are able to observe weaker growth in the left lung than in the right one, the organism itself uses that polar aspect of the vital forces to tell us the 'cause' for this asymmetry. The left lung is subject to a slightly greater extent to the life-hindering forces which come to full fruition in the upper human being; the right lung is marked to a greater degree by the vital lower organization of the human being. Thus the two polar principles in the human being, which have moved far apart in their one-sidedly developed centres, confront one another from above and below on the same level in the lung.

The division of the trachea into the right and left lung (right and left bronchus) fixes this directional contrast physiologically in the dynamic of its growth.

The right bronchus leads sharply downwards. The left one remains upwards to the left at a more acute angle. Many depictions do not reflect these angles as they really are in the living person since the artists or photographers modelled their work on samples taken from the thorax of the deceased. But clinical practice speaks a clear language about the different angles at which the trachea divides: the majority of foreign objects which end up in the trachea (above all with children) fall into the right bronchus.[135] It has developed more closely towards the vertical which the left bronchus has avoided. The element which makes thinking possible in the sensory and nervous system affects the development of the left lung to a greater extent; the element which comes to awareness from the metabolic and limb system as the will, influences the development of the right lung. Through this organ, then, human beings feel the conflict, the doubt, which forms the basis of their freedom.

The asymmetrical nature of human beings into a right side encompassing the will and a left side which represents a receptive, thinking quality, finds its archetype in the lung. There freedom develops in the equilibrium which the heart seeks between 'love of action' and the 'accommodation of the wants of others.' 'Life in the love of action and letting live in the accommodation of the wants of others,' Rudolf Steiner writes in Chapter Nine of his *Philosophy of Freedom,* 'is the fundamental maxim of free human beings.'

27. The expression of the middle human being

Let us now seek to understand the varying rates of lung development, the 2:3 of its divisions, through our understanding of music. Let us imagine that two strings, which have been tuned to reflect the fifth, oscillate and that the pitch of these two strings is lowered steadily while maintaining the interval of a fifth. Beyond the bass region the noise zone begins. If we imagine their oscillations as getting slower and slower we will in the end reach two rhythms which divide the same period of time in the proportion 2:3. The difference between rhythm and tone (melody) on a physical level consists merely of the difference in speed of the periodic process. Tone is greatly speeded up rhythm; rhythm greatly slowed down tone.

In studies of gait, it has been found that the period in which the foot touches the ground ('stance phase') has the proportion 61% to 39% with the period that it swings in the air without touching the ground ('swing phase') (Hoepke/Landsberger[136]). That is approximately 60%:40%. The proportion 3:2 thus appears in the rhythm of walking itself. As is to be expected, the 'two' (40%) goes together with the swing phase, during which the leg leaves the ground, and the 'three' with the stance phase, in which it is in contact with the ground. The growth dynamic which allows the lung to grow into its rhythmical functions turns, in the legs, into the rhythm of the muscles between stance and swing, between placing and carrying. Respiration is hidden in walking.

> In 1 you find the prime, the second in 9/8, the third in 5/4,
> the fourth in 4/3 and in 3:2 the fifth. The whole human
> being from inside out is a fifth, is constructed inwardly as a
> fifth. That is something which permeates the whole person.
> Those are the conclusions which a sculptural and musical
> anthropology leads up to (Steiner[137]).

The fifth is active in the force which keeps the centre of gravity in upright posture in an unstable state above the support axis of the region of the fourth. We understood this perception of the will in the muscular system as the fifth in which the 'attraction of freedom' can be felt; if it were absent the will would go to sleep.

We can feel the fifth not only as a melodic interval but also as the rhythm of the limbs if we walk this rhythm in a kind of dance step. And here the reader is requested to try it out since otherwise he or she will be missing the perceptions which are needed for our conceptual understanding of the process.

Example 31.

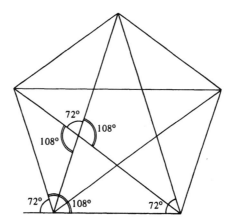

Figure 58.

In taking three steps forward and two steps back within the same time period (= minim) one can experience the 2:3 of the fifth in the dynamic with which the right lung strives forwards and outwards in three lobes while the two lobes of the left lung are restrained — 'will' on the right, 'reflection' on the left. If we learn to walk with the legs and their earth rhythm this drama of the divided soul's struggle for freedom on earth, we learn to comprehend the expression of the middle human being:

> Do you think that I have come to give peace on earth? No, I
> tell you, but rather division; for henceforth in one house
> there will be five divided, three against two and two against
> three (Luke 12:51f).

Thus speaks the cosmic master builder who enters his house so that the human being can achieve freedom, can realize his true nature. In Luke's Gospel the Word turned flesh of the lungs speaks the physical rhythm of the fifth. In the lung the Word separates the physical unity which is created by the blood so that the 'I' can take the place of the blood and recreate the unity anew.

> Thus the gospels are writings which have their origin in the
> wisdom which created human beings. Human beings reveal
> the spirit through their bodies; the gospels do the same
> through their writing ... Mankind is truly being guided if
> persons are active within it who write documents from the
> same sources which create the human being in wisdom
> (Steiner[138]).

Just as physical conception takes place in the region of the fifth, so the fruit of the human being's life on earth, freedom, matures through this interval. This comprehensive significance of the fifth in human beings is revealed in the geometry of the pentagram. The pentagon and the five pointed star demonstrate in all their angles the proportion 2:3, which appears as 72°:108°. The pentagram is the geometrical image of the fifth in the human shape. The expression of the middle human being — 'three against two, and two against three' — sounds as the fifth and sculpts the external form of the whole human being as we saw it grow into the pentagram in five steps (Figure 4) at the beginning of the book.

PART IV

Eurythmy as the Musical Structure of the Human Being Expressed as Movement

The movements of music eurythmy reveal outwardly what is inwardly concealed as human' physiology; we already saw this in the musical physiology of the parathyroid glands. In this Part the relationship of the inner musical structure to the movements of music eurythmy will be studied in detail.

28. Major and minor in the lung formation[139]

We have dealt with the dynamic which regulates the enhanced growth of the right lung and the retarded growth of the left lung in Part Three. The same quality is active here as in the polarity of arterial and venous blood. The dynamic of that out-streaming excess of our own life and will, and its opposite of being overwhelmed by the life of the world — this lives in the harmonic contrast of major and minor. Major and minor are to a certain extent the reflection in the inner harmonic feeling of the proportions which underlie the fifth and its dynamic. They are 'the continuation within of the experience of breathing' (see page 168). In the major mood we experience the musical image of that spiritual-musical impulse which is present in the formation of the right lung; in the minor there sounds, like a reflection, what flows through the soul-body in the formation of the left lung. With such musical impulses the soul-body penetrates the etheric body with sound. In artistic consciousness these impulses appear as in the musical theme which introduced us to the polarity of the venous and arterial blood (see page 32 and Examples 1-3).

The melodic phrase Mozart constructs out of the major third streams outwards in a convex shape; the movement flowing from the minor third streams constrictedly inwards. We experience the fashioning effect of the harmony (major–minor) in the spatial shape of the melodic phrase. This makes audible the way in which these harmonies with their objective creative forces drive the right lung outwards into the will, and hold back the left lung internally.

> The melodic element can be well compared with the sculptural element. The sculptural element is related, is it not, to space as is the melodic element to time. Anyone who has a keen sense for this temporal orientation will recognize that *a kind of temporal sculpture is contained in the melodic element. The melodic element corresponds to a certain extent to what sculpture is in the outer world.*[140]

We learn first of all to recognize the movements of the astral body in the musical realm, as they are reflected in our physical and etheric bodies. For this reason the pre-eminent organ of the musician is the lung, which forms the boundary between the etheric body in the blood, and the astral body which is at home in the air.

29. Sculptural-musical movements of the higher human members in eurythmy

Steiner used his perception to translate the movements which the etheric body carries out in playing or listening to music, (when it gives itself to the musical impulses of the astral body), into the movements of eurythmy, perceptible to the senses. Since these etheric movements originally generate and then control the movements of

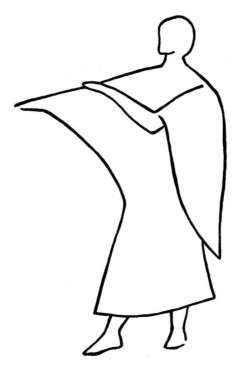

Figure 59. Sketch for the eurythmic gestures for the major chord.

growth of the organs, the question arises: do we discover a correspondence between the eurythmic movements for major and minor moods
given by Steiner out of his research and the sculptural movements of
the formation of the lungs, penetrated by these musical impulses? The
sequence of movements for the major and minor triads have something in common with the movements for the melodic major and
minor thirds, in that the major is formed by an extending movement,
and the minor by a bending movement. Steiner found:

> With every extension something proceeds from our will, and
> the surrounding aura brightens ... Extension carries the will
> out, releasing life-force ... With flexion, life-force is
> expended within ... [the human being] is inwardly consumed
> if he only flexes.[141]

The vital process, the musical movement and the basic eurythmic
gesture consequently correspond to the formative processes of the
right and left lungs. The details given for the major triad:[142]

C — 'stepping':   a step forwards to the right;

E — 'movement':   stepping is followed by an extending move-
                       ment of the right arm (palm facing outwards
                       or down);

G — 'form':   the left hand touches the right arm, bringing
                       the process to rest.

For the minor triad the following sequence of movements is given:

C — 'stepping':   a step backwards to the left;

E^b — 'movement':   the step is followed by a flexing of the left
                       arm, palm turned inwards, till the hand touches
                       the body;

G — 'form':   the right arm is led towards the left, and holds
                       the gesture of the left arm.

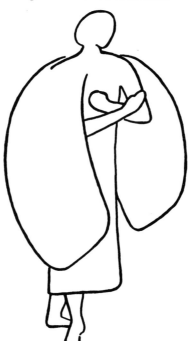

*Figure 60. Sketch for the
eurythmic gestures for the minor chord.*

Whereas Steiner employs expressions like 'thrusting' for the major gesture, he emphasized for minor that one should proceed from 'being really relaxed.' This entails a withdrawal of the will from muscular contraction, giving way to an impulse which grasps the human being from without. Our own life recedes before the universal life which lays hold of the human being.

The sequence of movements for the harmony of the major and minor chords is correspondingly metamorphosed for the pure melodic movements of the major and minor third.

Major third: extending the arm in pronation (palm of hand down) with the musical feeling of streaming out on the outer side of the upper arm over the elbow and ulna (ulna and radius are crossed).

Minor third: bending of the arm and opening of the hand (supination) with the feeling of the musical stream entering in from outside along the inner side of the arm over the radius (ulna and radius are parallel).

The eurythmic gestures for the major and minor triads reveal (to the right pressing forward in extension; to the left retracting in flexing) what the morphological movement of the growth of the lungs shows inwardly. This is emphasized when (as Steiner suggests) we study more closely the anatomy of the major extending motion and the minor flexing movement.

30. The anatomy of the major and minor gestures

The muscle for extending the forearm lies on the outer side of the upper arm and grasps the ulna at the elbow where the tendons begin (triceps). The most important muscle for flexing is the biceps. It lies on the inner side of the upper arm and it lays hold of the radius as its starting point. These tendons recoil with the turning in of the forearm (pronation), as for example when closing a door. If it actively contracts, the forearm flexor can also turn the forearm outwards

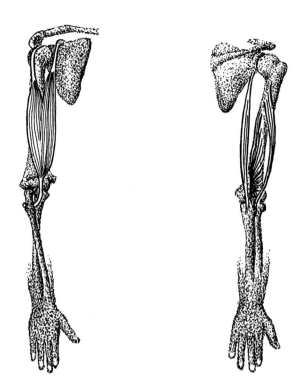

Figures 61 and 62. Musculus biceps (arm from the front)   (arm from behind)

(supination) as with opening a door. One can easily test this on oneself by feeling the right biceps with the left hand and strongly turning
the right forearm outwards, as with turning a key to open a lock. The
main flexor of the forearm also turns the palms upwards.

The extensor of the forearm, the triceps, is divided into three
'heads' (as its name suggests). The three parts pass to their common
tendon at the elbow from three different places on the upper arm and
shoulder-blade. (The biceps has two parts.) With the major chord we
stretch to the right with the three-part muscle lying on the outside.

With the minor chord we bend to the left with the two-part muscle
lying on the inside.[143] A glance back at the movement of the growth
of the lungs as they have become formed in the branching of the
wind-pipe (Figure 57) allows us to say: In the right bronchus an
extending movement of the etheric body is evident; in the left bron-

chus a flexing movement. The music eurythmy of the major and minor gestures outwardly reveals the musical impulses concealed in the chest which underlie lung development.

This sculptural-musical extension of the embryological development of the lungs suggests the question: Is there consequently a eurythmic gesture at the basis of the growth of the lungs in its dual nature? The musical pictures, embryonic forms of Imaginative and Inspirational knowledge, indicate the activity of spiritual beings. We gain an inkling of a eurythmy of divine creative beings.

> The human being is a finished form, as he stands before us
> ... This finished form has itself arisen out of archetypal
> forms which create and change ... How does my creator act
> in me as human being out of the essence of the worlds? If
> you want to find the answer, then you have to fashion the
> forms of eurythmy. God engages in eurythmy, and the result
> of this eurythmy is the human form. (Steiner[144]).

Consequently, a respect comes about for the spiritual essence of eurythmy, which awakens out of the union of science and art. Here the effective principle of eurythmy therapy also becomes recognizable in the widest sense: the sick person is encouraged to direct his limbs into those movements with which the divine spiritual beings formed his body before birth. In eurythmy therapy, the patient leads the earthly will of his limbs into the will of his higher, healing ego.

What we have discovered for the lungs can also be shown for the heart. We recall the minor-major process of the heart (page 35). The internalizing gesture of the minor mood also lives psychologically in the process of inhalation. This is the receiving physical side of breathing. But if we pursue in-breathing in its minor movement further inwards to its continuation in the blood, this internalization ends with the streaming in of the blood into the left ventricle of the heart. With the change of direction in systole, the blood streams major-like out of the heart to the periphery of the whole body. Here the physical function of the heart is experienced musically, continuing out of the in-breathing into the in-streaming phase of diastole. After a short standstill in the flow, the blood then changes direction and flows with will-like systole into the body. The constricting function of the heart (the only place in the body where the blood comes to a standstill) provides, as mentioned above, the possibility for the ego to enter, which can bring itself to consciousness through the interruption in the blood flow.

As they flow into the heart, the two streams of blood (one pouring into the right ventricle and the other into the left) flow approximately parallel. After the change of direction they cross over each other in leaving the ventricles of the heart. Here in the heart-beat we are given an archetypal picture of the eurythmic major-minor movement: the bones of the fore-arm placed parallel in the gesture for the minor, their crossed position in the gesture for the major are the visible movements of the the blood in the heart. The movement of the blood in the heart becomes the movement of the bones within the muscular covering of the forearm.

Figure 63.

In his lecture course on music eurythmy, Steiner translates the qualities of major and minor into the qualities of the vowels:

minor: A and E [ah and ay]

major: O and U [oh and oo]

In the change of harmony from minor to major and vice versa is the transitional quality of the vowel I [ee]. The ego's own sound holds the balance. In the functional cycle of the activity of blood activity this is that tenth of a second in which the blood goes through the death-

Figure 64. Apex of the heart.

moment of standstill. This ego-moment of cardiac activity is condensed into sculptural form in the moment of transition of both streams of blood in the apex of the heart. In the pattern of the heart muscle fibres, as they are sculpted embryonically by the blood, the static image of the ego stands before us.

Simplified, it becomes the symbol of the ego:

Figure 65.

31. The transition of the inner musical structure to music eurythmy

In Steiner's lecture course *Eurythmy as Visible Music,* music appears in the human being in two ways. In the third lecture we find the keynote (or the prime) in the activity of the feet, as we described in Chapter 18. In the seventh lecture the keynote appears in the collarbones.

As often when we meet such 'contradictions' in Steiner's work, we are dealing with two statements which are made from different points of view. They contradict each other as much as two photographs of a mountain which are taken from two different perpsectives 'contradict' each other. Both these viewpoints are clearly characterized by Steiner in the seventh lecture,[145] from which the other quotations are taken for this chapter, unless otherwise stated):

> I have often stressed that eurythmy is drawn from the nature
> of the structure and functions of the human being, from the
> possibilities of movement pre-figured in the human
> organism. The human organism on the one hand contains
> the musical element, which is in fact built into it, and on the

other hand (as should be especially mentioned in connection with music eurythmy) it contains music translated into movement. It will doubtless be obvious to you that the musical element is situated, so to speak, in the human chest structure, above the chest. If we put the question: How are we to find in the actual human structure the transition from singing, from the inner musical structure which lies at the basis of the human being, to the 'organism of movement' of eurythmy? — then, as is immediately apparent, we must turn to the limbs attached to the chest structure ...

On the one side there stands the 'inner musical structure which lies at the basis of the human being'; on the other side 'music translated into movement' — 'the "organism of movement" of eurythmy.' What we have contrasted as prime (the activity of the feet) with the octave (the activity of the head) and processes connected with the intervals found between — does not serve artistic presentation. It is music 'imprisoned' in the human being, the 'inner musical structure which lies at the basis of the human being.' For this the arms are adapted to reveal music through movement in space. Steiner now asks the question: 'How do we find the transition from the music which has created the human being out of the cosmos, which is effective in his organs, to eurythmic movement?' Much depends upon this question. For if this transition did not exist (or if it were not found) then the artistic justification for eurythmy would be missing. Only through such a transition is it possible that more is conveyed in the movement than the just personal feeling of the eurythmist. Such movement conveys more than the individualized musicality of the cosmos active in the organism. It is the excess of the musical creative force, which is available for artistic ends now that the organs are mature and no longer need to be formed. Only through such a transition can the limbs make visible in movement that which 'tunes' the organs afresh each night out of the harmonies of the spheres.

This transition was already to be seen in the way that the embryological development of the lungs was revealed in eurythmy in the major and minor triads. In spatial orientation and in the movements of the muscles, the major and minor triads in eurythmy shows right into the details the musical dynamic of the formation of the lungs through an image of movement. Nevertheless the outer movement and the inner organization remain side by side, even if they do mutually correspond. To understand the transition means to be able to answer the question: how does the original image cross over to its reflection; how do the inner, musically organizing forces find the way to eurythmic movement?

We are told that the bones and muscles at the base of the arm are directly related to those muscles which are attached from outside on to the larynx: 'In the surrounding muscles and bones of the arms and hands it is possible to trace something connected with voice production, with the initiating of the sound.' And the reference follows on that the root of the arm lies in the collar-bone directly adjacent to where the sound is initiated.

Steiner then takes the external observations a step further by describing the feeling which should be developed in the collar-bones.

The most necessary preparation for music eurythmy,
therefore, is a concentration of your consciousness to the
left and the right sides of the collar-bone. And when
beginning in music eurythmy, with the first step, [beim
auftreten], transfer your consciousness to the left and right
collar-bone. Feel that all the subtle possibilities of
movement which you pour into your arms and hands really
proceed from your collar-bone, just as the voice proceeds
from its starting point. Then feel that you pour this feeling,
which you consciously stimulate in the collar-bone, first into
the socket of the upper arm. And feel too when you express
the keynote with the legs, with the step, the following:
Already while only lifting the arm, the force which causes
the arm to be raised goes to the keynote from up here,
proceeding from the root of the arm.

Consciousness should be focussed in the collar-bone 'with the first step.' At the end of the quotation, this root in the collar-bone is compared to the expression of the keynote through stepping. Steiner consequently relates the origin of the keynote of the collar-bone to the activity of the feet. In the next lecture[146] we discover the explanation: 'The scale is the human being, but the human being in fact as he encloses his chest, or in so far as his chest is able to be revealed outwardly via the collar-bone.' 'The scale, which is the human being' was discussed in the third lecture[147] the prime manifests in the feet. The activity of the feet is a process of the prime; in the region of the throat the inner musical structure streaming from below upwards is expressed as transition in the octave of the head and in the octave of the word (see page 107). When we prevent the musical stream which begins in the activity of the feet 'with the first step' and which strives to become sound in the larynx from turning into song; when we suppress the activity of the larynx, then the inner musical structure can find its outer expression in another way: the change to visible singing of the arm movements. The inner musical structure meets its boundary in the seventh-process of the throat. It finds its outer expression in the octave of the collar-bone and the shoulder-blade. This octave becomes the keynote of music eurythmy. This is the reason for the instruction to feel the point of departure in the collar-bone 'with the first step;' in other words, in relationship to the activity of the feet. Consequently a way does exist to lay hold of the point of departure of music eurythmy in the collar-bone, by beginning with the experience of the keynote in the feet, and singing inwardly the scale of the human form up to the octave of the collar-bones.

Now we can answer the question posed at the beginning: 'How does the inner musical structure pass over to the movement of music eurythmy?' The inner music which lies at the basis of the human being arrives at its boundary in the seventh-region of the throat, where it turns into outer expression as singing. If the activity of the larynx is suppressed then the inner musical structure finds the transition over this threshold of the seventh to the octave of the collar-bones, to the new keynote of the 'music transformed into movement.' In September 1924, Steiner speaks of this octave to doctors and priests in the lecture course on pastoral medicine:

> The whole dynamic which weaves in the blood circulation
> and respiratory circulation is musically orientated, and you
> can only understand it when you think in musical forms.
> You can only understand it when, for example, you perceive
> in the skeleton what has streamed into it as creative forces,
> which then in rarified form are active in the breathing and
> in the circulation, but according to formative forces which

> are musical. We can almost see how the mood of the octave
> proceeds backwards from the shoulder-blades as far as the
> root of the bones of the upper arm and we find the second
> in the bones of the upper arm ...[148]

Proceeding from within, Steiner speaks of the octave of the shoulder-blade. For the eurythmic movement, passing to the upper arm, this octave becomes prime in the shoulder-blades. The ensuing description corresponds to that of the lecture course on music eurythmy. The octave of the music (which has created the human form), becomes prime in the music transformed into movement. The human being engaged in eurythmy moves in a higher octave than the bodily organization lying beneath it. To feel this inwardly 'with the first step,' as the musical 'tuning' of the instrument, gives the orientation for the point of departure in the shoulder-blade and collar-bone.

Three octaves proceed from the seventh-region of the throat: the sculptural octave of the head, the musical octave of the collar-bone and shoulder-blades, and the speech octave of the word.

Already in the previous chapter we saw the arm as the external expression of the lungs. Now we can understand how the inner structure passes over into the outer: we have to produce a plastic-musical inversion. At the end of the lecture course on music eurythmy Steiner points more than once to this inversion, and we shall now turn to this in detail in the following chapters:

> Everything arising from the lungs, larynx, and so on, when
> metamorphosed and suitably projected outwards, is reflected
> in the association of collar-bone — the shoulder-blade
> concludes the process — collar-bone, shoulder-blade, upper
> arm, forearm, and the bones of the fingers.[149]

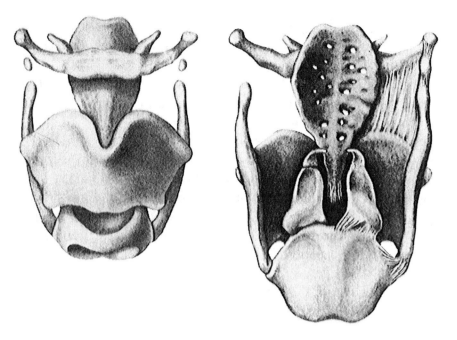

Figure 66a. Larynx from in front   *Figure 66b. Larynx from behind*
(From: Berendes, Link, Zollner, Hals-Nasen-Ohren-Heilkunde).

32. The inversion of the lungs and the larynx into the arms

The collar-bone is passively moved by the muscles attached to the shoulder-blade.

> It is precisely the collar-bone movements which are most dependent on the movements of the other two bones [shoulder-blade and upper arm], and for this reason the collar-bone, not without some justification, is compared (despite its own particular muscles) to a meniscus;* the

* Meniscus: disc-shaped transitional cartilage, for instance in the knee-joint, where it purely passively mediates between the movement of the thigh and the calf.

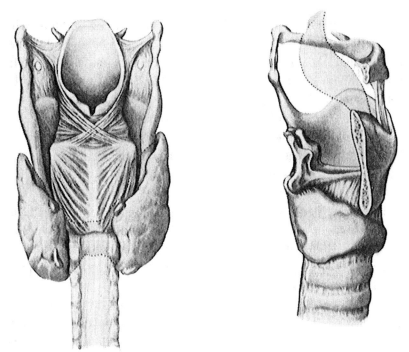

Figure 67. Muscles of the larynx. a *From behind.* b *From the side.*

collar-bone does not move of its own accord; it is almost
entirely raised or shifted by the shoulder-blade ... Independent movements of the collar-bone without primary or
secondary accompanying movements of the shoulder-blade
do not arise, even with the movement of breathing.[150]

The shoulder-blade is completely immersed in muscles. Its concave
front surface, lined with muscle, slides to and fro on the rib-cage and
carries the socket of the upper arm into the position from which the
desired arm movement can commence. A comparable picture is given
in the larynx: the vocal cords are two muscular cords in apposition to
each other, which form the edges of two tent-shaped sheets of muscle.

The vocal cords are fixed in front on the thyroid cartilage, the
Adam's apple. Behind they are both attached to each of the four ends
of the two tetrahedally-formed arytenoid cartilages. This adjusting

cartilage is surrounded by numerous tiny muscles which with lightning-like pushing and sliding movements move hither and thither on the annular, or cricoid cartilage. Their seventh-movement in the activity of the larynx, breaking away from the body, is emphasized by Hermann Braus:

> The phonetic movement is only possible by breaking the contact between the surfaces (in the joint between the adjusting cartilage and the annular, or cricoid cartilage) ... In the phonetic movement the adjusting cartilage is thus held suspended by the muscles.[151]

The vocal cords themselves are largely passive in the sense of external muscle movement. Stretched between the adjusting cartilage and the Adam's apple, their function is essentially regulated by the adjusting cartilage and also by the tilting movement of the Adam's apple. Nevertheless the muscles of the vocal cords are also extremely mobile! They oscillate to the frequency of the respective sound. The inner musical structure thus turns into the outer, physically sounding muscle in the larynx. Eurythmy retains, intensified and developed, what is achieved in this initiating of the voice: muscles are set into musical movement, which however is carried out in space.

Against this background, we can understand the transformation between the two anatomically comparable organic regions: The vocal cords are transformed into the collar-bones. The two tetrahedrally-formed arytenoid cartilages are transformed into the two triangular surfaces of the shoulder-blades (Gisbert Husemann). The Adam's apple is transformed into the upper part of the breastbone (Manubrium sterni).

Every further step inwards becomes in the arm a further step outwards. The wind-pipe flexibly attached to the preceding parts with its articulating cartilage, becomes the upper arm with its head-joint. This is in contact with the shoulder-blade and collar-bone as the annular cartilage is with the adjusting cartilage and vocal cords, whose lateral tent as Conus elasticus extends to the annular cartilage.

Now the wind-pipe branches into the two main bronchial tubes. We already recognize their major and minor nature from the discussion of lung embryology. The right bronchial tube becomes the ulna, while the left is transformed into the radius.

The root of the lung (hilus) becomes the carpus, or base of the hand. Here we stand within and without at the nodal point from which everything branches out. The lymph nodes, concentrated in the lungs at this point, store throughout the whole of life the bits of matter in the air, the dust, which could damage the blood. The lungs of coal-miners contain lymph nodes which are filled with black coal dust. If such a lymph node is removed in an operation and is cut by the surgeon's scalpel, the mineral dust caught and concentrated there from the inhaled air makes a grating noise. We are in the sphere of the fourth.

The extension into space of the five lobes of the lungs leads to the fifth, which we already know as the proportion of the lung 2:3. In the hand, the five bones of the middle of the hand, the metacarpal bones, appear as the instrument of the eurythmic fifth (see Figure 68).

With the sixth the musical space and the eurythmic movement expands. On the way inwards, we move out of the realm of the air of the fifth into the warm stream of the inner expanse of the blood in the lungs, which flows through an area up to seventy square metres. The eurythmic movement expands into the periphery. This expansion becomes physically visible through the spreading of the metacarpal-phalangeal joints are spread (what Steiner calls the 'lower finger' is anatomically the proximal phalanx of the finger, what he calls 'upper finger' is the middle phalanx and distal phalanx of the finger). By going beyond the boundary of our physical form, the fifth, the physical reflections of the inversion also become less evident; the important thing increasingly becomes the movement and ever less the physical limb. If we proceed inwards, then we arrive at the constricted flow by which the blood flows at high velocity from the surface of the lungs into the left side of the heart through the pulmonary veins. This appears outwardly as the gesture for the seventh. The streaming of the blood into the heart itself is eurythmically the movement for the octave. In terms of projective geometry, the centre is the point which reflects the infinitely distant plane.[152]

The one cardio-respiratory organism turns into two arms through inversion. In this the octave appears to double — 1:2 — seen as external proportion.

In this way the octave of the collar-bones also bears witness to the power of the ego to re-embody, spiritually re-enlivened through

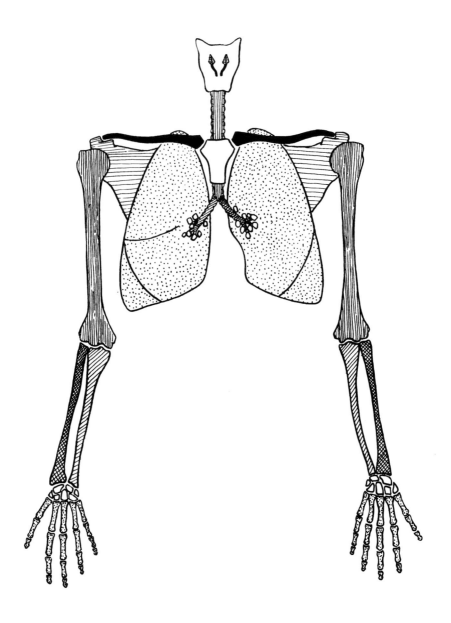

Figure 68. The inversion of lung and larynx in the arm and the hand.

inversion, that which was freed from the body in dying, as we have already experienced this power in the octave of the head and in the octave of the word. The ego's macrocosmic breathing process of incarnation and excarnation, spanning the millennia, is reflected in these three octaves as the microcosmic physiology of the ego-organization.

33. The laws at work in music eurythmy therapy

We recall the significance of breathing for the formative impulses of the whole human being. Breathing, discussed in Part Three, became for us the sculptural-musical creative movement of the etheric body. Every function and form of an organ can be conceived as a metamorphosis of a breathing movement, of a movement of expansion and invagination. The lungs continuously heal the human being by purifying him in exhalation from the illnesses of the blood, and intensify in inhalation the cosmic forces of his origin. The lungs are the actual 'Mercury' in the human being.

From this it is understandable why Steiner in his music eurythmy course explained the healing effects of music eurythmy through the inversion of the lungs into the arms:

When you now consider the intimate connection between eurythmy and the whole structure and function of the human being, it will no longer seem strange to you that in the case of music eurythmy too (although perhaps with occasional variations) we are able to speak of a eurythmy therapy. Only think of all that lies behind what I have discussed today! We have realized that there is both an inner and outer organization in the formation of arms and hands. They fit each other as the nut to a nutshell; they are built up from the same forces. Consequently, if we have to treat a diseased lung, it is possible to work on this lung by

encouraging the patient to do music eurythmy in a certain
way as eurythmy therapy ... For the whole muscular and
bony structure of hand and arm is in reality nothing but an
outer, concave image of what exists in inner, convex form
in the lungs; and indeed, proceeding further, in the heart,
and everything concerned with speaking and singing right
out as far as the lips.[153]

The previous Part was completely devoted to the course taken by
this seventh lecture. It begins with the question: How does the inner
musical structure turn into the instrument of music eurythmy? And it
concludes with the inversion into the arms of the cardio-respiratory
system. This is the answer and at the same time the effective principle
of music eurythmy therapy. We will now investigate the significance
of this inversion for illness and healing in the light of the sculptural
exercise which occupied us as image of the sculptural and musical
stream in Chapter 3.

The sculptural stream of inhalation carries the excess of life, which
we feel as the active strength of the limbs. Exhalation awakens
consciousness in using up this sculptural element.

In the course of the previous Parts it became clear that we have
before us here the dual nature of the astral body, which at night is in
harmony with the sculptural stream of the etheric body, and during the
day resists this stream. Inhalation retains something of the quality of
the nocturnal side of the astral body for all those organs in which we
normally do not develop consciousness; in other words, those that also
sleep by day. In exhalation, the day side of the astral body dominates.
We termed this contrast the 'Abel music' of the sleeping human being
and the 'Cain music' of the awake human being.

Music eurythmy comes about when the music which is liberated
and brought to consciousness in the degenerative stream does not
sound physically in the larynx, but is inverted into the musical place
of origin of the shoulder girdle. Thereby our musical experience
streams out of the shoulder girdle into the arms, which means it
moves in harmony with the sculptural stream of the etheric body, as
it manifests outwardly in the flow of the arterial blood and in the form
of the bones (see page 226). The inversion process occurs when the
music, freeing itself from the degenerative process, changes direction

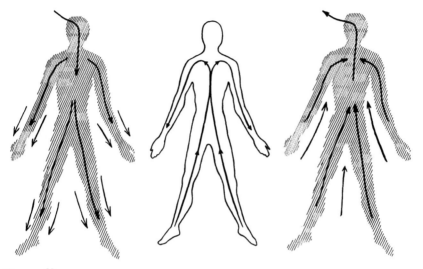

Figure 69.

and no longer moves *against* but *with* the sculptural stream. The ego lays hold of the astral body and inverts it into its cosmic, healing relationship to the physical-etheric body. It conveys the nocturnal condition of the human constituent elements into the wakened will of the day. (This effective principle of music eurythmy therapy will emerge more clearly in the next chapter, especially with reference to the major and minor movements.)

34. The human arm as musical sculpture

34.1 The human arm in the organism of time

The movement of the legs allows our body to change its position in space. If we remain standing in one place then another movement can be observed, the movement of breathing. This does not result in an advance through space; it is the movement of the muscles and bones directed inwards from external space to the life-processes of the blood.

The flow of the blood itself with the heart as its centre is an enclosed, circular movement in time. As the muscles of the limbs move in exterior space, so do the muscles of breathing and of the heart move in time.

The arms are freed of their spatial constriction by the human upright posture. A comparison with the spatially bound fore-limbs of animals shows how the human arms functionally are completely made part of the breathing as a temporal organism. Even when the arms move in space, the impulse for the movement originates from the temporal organism of heart and lungs. This was shown by the inversion of the embryological development and the finished form of the lungs into eurythmic-musical movement. In this chapter we shall discuss in detail the musical structure of the arms. In order to do this, however, we will approach the arms once more from a comprehensive point of view.

We can understand the development of the wing of a bird, the pectoral fins of a fish, or the forelegs of hoofed animals, an ibex for instance, by asking in what realm of nature the animal lives. The concept of adaptation shows in reality that it is the biotopes which out of the variety of genetically possible forms produced those which it can sustain in life. The air forms the birds' wings, as the water produces the fins and the rock the forelegs of the ibex. These elements intrude their own laws on the creation of the animals' organism, so that the animal is overpowered by them. It is confined in that element. Air penetrates the bird right into the bones of the upper arm, where it replaces the marrow. The bones of the upper-arm of most birds engage in an exchange of gases like the sinuses of our nose. Similarly the soft earth comes to expression in the mole's digging hand, water in the fish's fins, and the ground of the steppes in the hoof of the zebra.

When in comparison we ask the same question about the human hand — out of which element of the realms of nature can it be understood: out of the earth, the water or the air? — we find no answer. The human arm cannot be understood from this point of view because it is not governed from outside. Just for this reason the arm can be the instrument for the expression of inner life in manifold ways: in handwriting, hand pressure, gesture, in the personal style of a sculptor, painter or musician. The human arm does not reflect nature which leaves its impression in the animal; through the upright posture the arm is lifted out of this effect and is free to express the soul within. Consequently the arm is a picture of human freedom out of which the human being can take a tool in his hand and lay it down again, enter a car or aeroplane and leave it again. Man's tools and vehicles are creations of his inner life and of his hands.

The comparison of the animals' forelegs with the human arm shows that the latter as an archetype stands very close to the animal limbs. In the embryonic state, they more or less clearly pass through a preliminary stage which corresponds to the human form, but then surpass it. The human arms themselves are therefore the expression of the creating archetype which in the animal kingdom develops metamorphoses stamped by the outer world. We conceive a characteristic feature of the structure of the human ego when we see how the human being embodies the archetype of the various parts of the body; an archetype which in the ego-less animals is driven into different metamorphoses by the forces of nature.

The creative archetype in the arm awakens in the human being as an idea, and can be turned 'manually' — mechanically and technologically — into all the forms of movement present in the animals. Our technological advances are consequently to a high degree repetitions and intensifications of animal achievements (submarine, boat, car, aeroplane, and so on).

The legs move in space; heart and lungs move in time. When we take a look at the actual activity of the head, thinking, then we see no movement at all. In concepts we move free of time in so far as we are able arbitrarily to call to mind things of the future or the past. Consequently thinking is a movement outside space and time. It has to be so, because in thinking space and time become conscious, and we can only become conscious of that from which we have separated ourselves. If thinking itself were a process proceeding completely in time, we would not be able to be conscious of time itself. Only the appearance of thinking is an occurrence in time. Its essence is beyond space and time, because it produces both of these concepts as forms of consciousness. A movement beyond space and time can be called a movement in eternity. Our conclusions thus appear as follows:

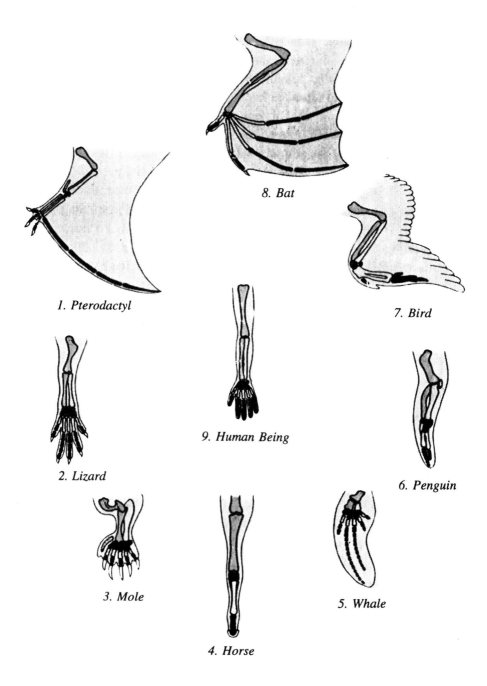

Figure 70. The human arm as prototype of the limbs of animals.

thinking	movement in eternity
breathing/heart-beat	movement in time
walking	movement in space

The arms are attached to the inner temporal organism of the chest organs; they are organs of expression and of will for the inner soul and spirit of the human being. What is the movement corresponding to their nature? Which movement purely occurring in time is the expression of the soul? This is musical movement. In the arms the human organism is able to transfer the movement of music (which occurs purely in time) into space, in other words the possibility for musical eurythmy.

34.2 The collar-bone

We observe on the living person the form of the arm as a whole with regard to the sculpting movements of the etheric body. The shoulder shows the three-dimensional fullness of deltoid muscle, which, like an extended sphere, extends into the upper arm. In the forearm we note a tapering and with the transition into the hand, where the form (entirely three-dimensional till then) tends to change into a two-dimensional, flat body. Here the bony skeleton forms contours below the skin. The indentation between the fingers is clearly continued on the back and palm of the hand as concave surfaces. The muscles which give the fingers strength have completely retreated to the fore-arm. The fingers acquire their strength through 'remote control.' The fingers themselves are free of muscles; instead of these they have the highly developed sense of touch. When we recall that the turning of a key requires the biceps which begin on the shoulder-blade, it becomes clear that in the shoulder and upper-arm next to the torso the strength of the arm dominates; outside in the hand its sensory activity predominates.

Linking up to our introductory sculptural thoughts in Chapter 2, we follow the arm from within outwards and discover that the forms of the arm begin convex and young at the shoulder, and become more concave and older towards the outside.

Let us now observe the collar-bone, as a whole and then in its parts. Inside fully three-dimensional, on the outer end flattening out; inside soft, bold, young forms, on the outer end highly differentiated, hard, ancient forms. The collar-bone appears like a reduced image of the whole arm (G. Husemann[154]).

Fully developed collar-bones show, in the direction of the upper-arm, a clear indentation into which the acromion of the shoulder-blades nestles. A clear indentation is to be seen on the underside too, towards the outer end. (Since the collar-bone finishes its ossification very late, we frequently find an indentation on the inner end too, which comes from the fact that the epiphysis has become lost. With completed ossification the inner end of the collar-bone is predominantly convex, with at most a minimal depression.) The anatomist Waldeyer shows in his doctorate thesis that the joint between the breast-bone and the collar-bone functionally corresponds to a ball and socket joint.[155] Here the depression in the breast-bone is the socket, and the inner end of the collar-bone is the (more or less) hypothetical ball.

The collar-bone is the potential whole arm, resting concealed in the body, not yet appearing in external movement; musically speaking it is a prime, which goes on to reveal its essence as movement of the whole arm, in the octave.

front

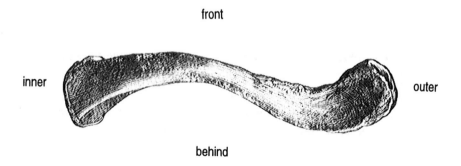

inner   outer

behind

Figure 71. Right collar-bone from above.

34.3 The moulding of the collar-bone

Using the limb-exercise the collar-bone comes about in four steps:

Figure 72.

After experiencing with the fundamental sculptural and musical forces in the earlier chapters we can directly understand Steiner's description of the musical forces effective in the collar-bone. In the seventh lecture of the course on music eurythmy he places them in the context of the whole arm:

> The form of that part of the collar-bone which tends outwards will give you the feeling that it is receiving something, that it allows things from outside to approach it. In that part which goes out from the middle [from the breast-bone,] you will feel an out-streaming tendency. In the collar-bone you really do have two streams, one flowing outwards, the other inwards. The outward stream passes through the back part of the arm, down the ulna to the back of the hand. The inward stream goes through the palm of the hand, up the radius and back again to the collar-bone. Here two streams continually move, one flowing upwards in this way, and the other outwards. The one gives something, whereas the other is receptive. This approach leads directly to a real understanding of the major and minor moods.

We recall the physiological correlates which we found for these 'streams': the streams of the arterial and venous blood; the positions and functions of the flexors and extendors. The music of the entire human being also lives in the part, in the collar-bone, as the major and minor streams, which have produced its three-dimensional form.

34.4 Prime and keynote in the collar-bone

As in the activity of the feet, the whole body is braced in the keynote of the scale, so the arm finds its bracing on the breastbone. Anatomically the interclavicular ligament links both collar-bones. Without this bond, in a sideways bending of the torso, for example, the shoulder of the raised side would sink down. With every movement it holds both collar-bones so they lie level in relation to one another and at right angles to the backbone or breastbone. The eurythmist experiencing the region of the prime in the shoulder girdle, takes up the reflecting harmonization of the collar-bones in the horizontal and their crossing point with the vertical axis.

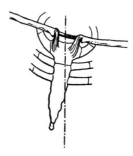

Figure 73. The interclavicular ligament (linking the collar-bones) when the left shoulder has been lowered.

The movement which runs over the breastbone from one collar-bone to its mirror-image, is musically the movement of the sound which meets itself, the prime as [melodic] interval. When the prime is felt as a degree of the scale (keynote), from which another intervallic movement moves away, then the movement streams out from the middle towards both sides.

With regard to its ossification, the collar-bone assumes a special position amongst all the bones. It is the first bone which begins to harden in the life of the embryo. But its ossification lasts longest of all the bones, coming to its end only in the second decade of life. Thus it encompasses the whole development of the human skeleton (Woernle[156]).

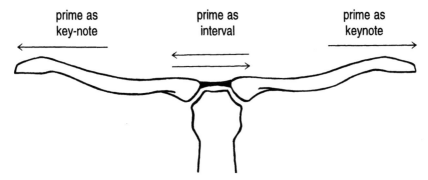

Figure 74. Prime as interval and as keynote

In conclusion there follows a report on a conference about the collar-bone.[157]

Gisbert Husemann valued the fact that in Steiner's lecture course on music eurythmy the point of departure of the gestures for the intervals was based on a detailed scientific, comparative-anatomical description of the collar-bone, and found this to be characteristic of the new unity of science and art found in anthroposophy. On the basis of these ideas the human collar-bone was observed through the various metamorphoses of bones in the animal species. The richer the mobility of the fore-limbs of an animal, the more significant is the swing of the

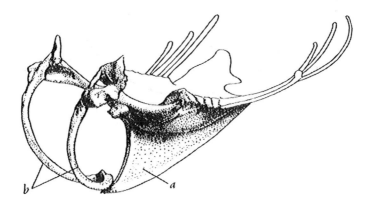

Figure 75. Collar-bones of the storm petrel a = breastbone, b = collar-bones

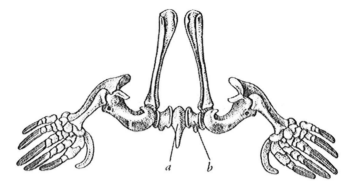

Figure 76. Collar-bones of a mole, a = breastbone, b = collar-bones

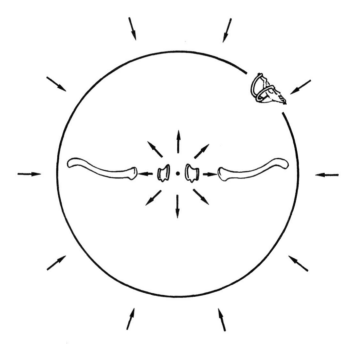

Figure 77. The collar-bones of the mole in sphere of influence of the central forces; the collar-bones of the storm petrel in the forces of the periphery; that of the human being as forming the balance between these extremes.
(After Gisbert Husemann).

collar-bone over the chest. This was studied on models of the bones of a storm petrel, a kite, a pelican and other creatures. It was seen on a model skeleton of a mole how, in comparison to the creatures given over to the widths of space, the collar-bones under the earth appeared to be compressed. Here only two tiny square blocks could be seen.

The life of such oceanic birds in the sculptural forces of the earth's periphery is emphasized through the length of their journeys around the globe. The greater storm petrel (Puffinus gravis) moves twice every year from the South Atlantic (Tristan da Cunha) to beyond the Arctic Circle. The flight distance in other words practically encircles the earth once a year.[158]

This polarity of the widely extended arc of the soaring birds and the concentrated form of the collar-bone of the mole, which digs in the earth, was the starting-point from which modelling the human collar-bone under the direction of Reimar von Bonin commenced. In the human being's form both extremes are brought into balance. It becomes heavy at the inner end beginning at the breastbone. The outer end swings out, sensitively receding, towards the upper-arm. Starting with a ball of clay, we caused it to stretch, making towards the periphery. To the extent that the form tapers, it becomes sensitive and receptive. In this way one can experience sculpturally the whole human being in one small part: on the inside the collar-bone tends to concentrate will-like — opening like the senses outwards at the shoulder-joint; and in a swinging S-form in the middle it balances between both these activities.

The step to a musical understanding of these creative gestures was given through a remark of Goethe's. He wrote to Schlosser on February 19, 1815, that the major 'urges human nature ... towards the periphery,' and the minor 'urges into the subject,' ... 'engenders concentration in every way.' Laying hold of the inner, musical gestures of the astral body in the formation of the collar-bone was practised under the direction of Maria Schüppel.

If we turn our feeling for language to these sculptural-musical processes, then the receiving gestures of the collar-bone, open to the periphery, appear as the experience of 'A' ['ah']. The full form, streaming outwards, of the inner part of the collar bone at the breast-bone appears like the expression of 'O' ['oh']. And in the change from inwards to outwards and outwards to inwards, both interpenetrating, the 'I' ['ee'] arises as gesture of the middle movement. In the corresponding lesson with Wilfried Hammacher the sound-formation of the collar-bone was practised. Hammacher then showed how the movement of the collar-bone from outside inwards lives in the form of the poem *Nachtgeräusche* by C.F. Meyer. It begins completely with external sense-perceptions, with the barking of dogs and the striking of the clock in the church tower. Then the movement is internalized in a dialogue between two people. Then, in the middle of the poem, pure stillness reigns. Still further inwards the Imagination of the activity of breathing and of the heart appears, the latter in the murmuring of a spring, in the stroke of an oar. The poem appears to have arrived where the collar-bone rests on the breathing rib-cage above the heart.

Nachtgeräusche

Melde mir die Nachtgeräusche, Muse,
Die ans Ohr des Schlummerlosen fluten!
Erst das traute Wachtgebell der Hunde,
Dann der abgezählte Schlag der Stunde,
Dann ein Fischer-Zwiegespräch am Ufer,
Dann? Nichts weiter als der ungewisse
Geisterlaut der ungebrochnen Stille,
Wie das Atmen eines jungen Busens,
Wie das Murmeln eines tiefen Brunnens,
Wie das Schlagen eines dumpfen Ruders,
Dann der ungehörte Tritt des Schlummers.

(C.F. Meyer)

[Tell me, Muse, of the noises of the night which flood up to the ear of those who cannot sleep! — First the familiar watchful barking of the dogs, then the counted striking of the hour, then two fishermen talking on the shore, and then? Nothing, except the indistinct ghostly sound of unbroken stillness, like the breathing of a youthful breast, like the

murmuring of a deep spring, like the beat of a muffled oar,
— then the unheard step of sleep.][159]

We proceed along the path from the awake senses to the sleep of
the will. In the centre the ego experiences itself in the 'unbroken
stillness' *[ungebrochnen Stille]*. In the laws which form him, the
human being creates the true work of art and so reveals them.

34.5 The upper arm

Steiner's arrangement of the intervals on the arm becomes illumined
through the sculptural-musical canon of forms. The ball and socket
type of the shoulder, which is shown not only in the muscular relief
of the living arm but also by the head of the humerus, still belongs to
the sphere of the prime. The expanding movement of the second
dominates the humerus itself. The third produces the invagination in
the lower arm, through which the radius and ulna arise. We see before
us as the fundamental sculptural-musical form of shoulder, upper arm
and lower arm, that which makes the individual anatomical forms
musically comprehensible.

The sculptural surface of the upper arm shows a screwlike turned
surface which proceeds from the head of the upper arm to the elbow-
joint. It is not present with a new-born baby, and only comes about
gradually when the child learns to bring together both hands to a
middle line when grasping an object or its own tiny hands.

Figure 78. The basic sculptural form of the upper arm and lower arm

This rotation comes about in our development at the same time as
upright posture is achieved. In drawing upright the shoulder-blades
move out of their sideways position backwards to the back. The whole

rib-cage is moved backwards. The child's weight thereby becomes balanced in the axis of the upright position. But thereby the surfaces of the joints of the shoulder-blades turn towards the side. Through drawing the hands together, the upper arm turns in itself by about 90 degrees. This twisting, then, reflects the achievement of upright posture (G. Husemann). This can be demonstrated in the progression from animal to human being. Figure 79 shows the upper arm, drawn with the direction of its axis as seen from the head *a*: human foetus, eight weeks old, *b*: monkey (Cynocephalus), *c*: Neanderthal man, *d*: modern adult human being.

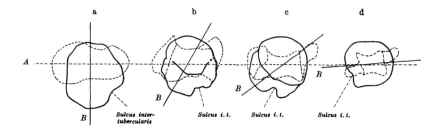

Figure 79. Turning of the humerus (upper arm). (From: Braus, Anatomie, I).

What is shown in the upper arm as the three-dimensional turning of the surface, becomes in the lower arm a free, internally structured turning of the radius and ulna (after G. Husemann). The step from the second to the third lives in this. The plantlike, sculptural activity of the outwardly-manifested second, unfolds to the inwardly free soul-movement of the third. Mozart fashions the beginning of the well-known Sonata in C major out of these free forces. The first four bars are composed out of the mood of the the third. Because the soul breathes completely in each melodic step, the theme maintains its tranquility despite the allegro. With the beginning of the flow of seconds in running scales, the possibility of breathing between the single notes disappears. Now sculptural life streams along so that the soul follows the movement from the outside. And only where thirds in this tempo appear in the bass is the soul inwardly drawn into the movement.

Example 32. Mozart, Piano Sonata K.545

The outer life of the second, which cannot yet be inwardly taken hold of by the sentient body in the same way as the third, becomes especially clear with trills. In the following theme by Beethoven, the activity of second and third confront each other directly. 'Breathing' and 'flowing,' feeling of inner space and the outer sculptural moving over the surface, meet:

Example 33. Beethoven, Piano Sonata, Op.27, No.1

34.6 The lower arm

We have studied the formative impulses of the intervals in musical works of art. We find them again in the relationship of the sculptural, outer twisting of the surface of the upper arm to the inwardly stuctured turning of the lower arm. The association of the major and the minor with the ulna and radius was already discussed in a different connection. The radius receives nearly the whole wrist at its lower joint. When we catch a ball or support the weight of our body when falling, it is the radius which receives that which reaches the lower arm via the hand. In other words, the radius receives what comes to meet the human being out of the world; it is functionally active in the sense of the musical minor movement. The ulna, with its connection to the upper arm, guides in predominantly stretching, outwardly directed movements towards the hand. The throwing of a ball is predominantly an activity of the ulna; the catching of a ball is predominantly an activity of the radius.

In the following illustration of the elbow-joint the power of the major mood of the ulna and the minor stream coming from outside in the radius can be seen especially clearly.

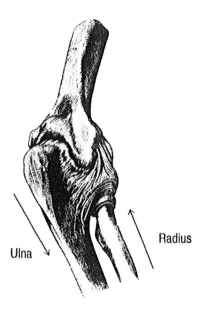

Figure 80. The elbow-joint.

The major movement can be intensified as at the beginning of Bruckner's Seventh Symphony:

Example 34.

Such an impulse imagined as a creative movement in the animal kingdom produces the Imagination of a bird. The major beings of the feathered world possess fore-limbs which are no longer able to receive, but can only fly. And when we have achieved enough confidence in sculptural-musical thinking, then we are able to answer without hesitation (without ever having dissected a bird) the question on which bone of the lower arm the flight feathers commence on the bird wing: obviously on the ulna. It is substantially stronger than the radius, especially with birds that fly. Birds are carried in the air by the stream of the major mood.

The other extreme is incorporated by the animals which have completely projected their fore-limbs to receive the gravity of the earth, the hoofed animals. With a horse the ulnae in the region of the wrist are completely retarded, and the weight is taken by the radii, the bones of the minor mood. The ulnae only sit as residue at the upper end, forming the joint with the upper arm.

In this way the fore-limbs of the hoofed animals contrast as extreme 'minor creations' with the fore-limbs of the birds as extreme 'major creations.'

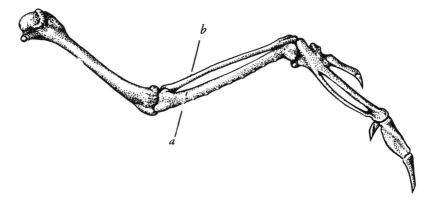

Figure 81. Ulna and radius of a dove. Notice the growth points of the feathers on the ulna (a = ulna; b = radius).

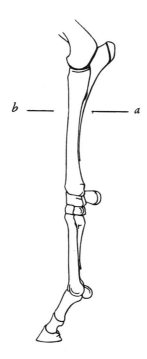

Figure 82. Shoulder and limb of the horse (a = ulna; b = radius).

The comparison of the flying action of two sorts of birds can provide more insight into the musical organization of the arm. A humming-bird, whirring around a flower — is one picture. A pelican, gliding over the water, with the calm, harmonious beat of its wings — is another picture. The eye, trained by music eurythmy for visible music, sees the seventh which shimmers in the humming-bird. In the movement of the pelican, we see the intervals of the lower tetrachord, for instance the second or third.

These musical 'motion images' appear in the skeleton, brought to rest, as sculpture:

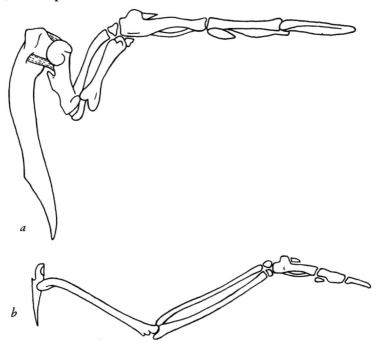

Figure 83. Skeleton of the arm of a humming bird (a) and of a Pelican (b), adjusted to equal length. (From Starck, Vergleichende Anatomie, Vol.II).

In Figure 83 the limb skeleton of a humming-bird and a pelican are adjusted to the same size. We see how with the humming-bird the fingers ray out extremely enlarged. We find the buttress for this extreme seventh structure in a correspondingly enlarged shoulder-blade, a prime-bone. In comparison the forearm and lower arm are

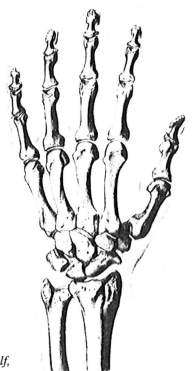

*Figure 84. Left hand, external (dorsal)
view of the skeleton. (From Benningholf,*
Lehrbuch, *Vol.I).*

retarded. The pelican on the other hand shows especially harmonious upper and lower arms, which give evidence of the second and third mood of its astral body.

That which the human being freely brings to expression as his capacity of soul is bound to the organism in the animal. This music is tied to the body with the animal; with human beings it is free in the soul. As eurythmists they can move as quick as lightning 'from pelican to humming-bird.'

34.7 The wrist

The physiological quality of the fourth consists in the force of solidification, which we found in the ripening of seeds, in the force of physical incarnation which is active in the process of birth, and also

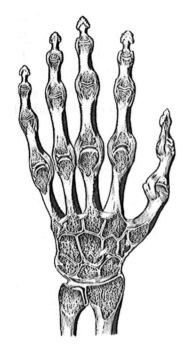

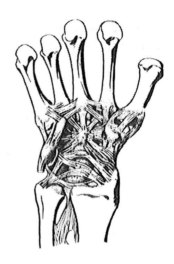

Figure 85. Left hand.
The joints have been
opened dorsally.

Figure 86. Ligaments of the base of
the right hand. Skeleton viewed from
palm volar (without fingers).

in the separation of the organism into single reproductive cells. Let us examine the region in which the fourth is presented in eurythmy. It has already been mentioned that the wrists, as part of the arms hanging down under the influence of gravity, are positioned somewhat below the hips, that is in the region of the male reproductive organs. The skeleton of the wrist reflects the quality of the fourth in its skeletal structure. It accords with the physically incarnating strength of this interval, that it is clearly and visibly expressed in the skeleton as no other interval is. The movement of the bones among themselves is suppressed. Instead of this the bones are interlinked through the strength of the semitone into a suggestion of a wall which is braced by the ligaments. The anatomist Braus, names the cube as the basic geometrical form of the bones of the wrist.

The correlate in the soul for this process of concentration in the fourth is waking up. The ego awakens into the region of the soul, which has been created by the third. The physical forces of concentration inspired Wagner in the scene in *Das Rheingold* where the giants Fafner and Fasold demand their wages from Wotan for building the castle of the gods. In the words of Fasold: *'stauten starken Stein wir auf'* ['heaped up strong rocks'] and *'Dort steht's, was wir stemmten'* ['there it stands, what we heaved up'] — the etheric-physical effect of the fourth is directly spoken about.

Example 35. Wagner, from Das Rheingold.

Edmund Pracht has pointed out that the missing fourth lends the pentatonic scale its suspended mood.[160] As mentioned in the chapter on the rib-cage, the soul of the child lives in the mood of the fifth up to its ninth year. This means that it still lives more outside the physical-etheric body than within it. After this it moves in and takes hold of the physical-etheric body from within, which then leads to puberty.[161]

These results of Steiner's musical study of the human being completely agree with the findings advanced by natural science. Let us now take up again the work of Suchantke and Pracht (page 96).

With a new-born infant none of the bones of the wrist have ossified; it merely consists of cartilaginous rudiments. Only around the ninth year have all the bones of the wrist ossified (with girls around the seventh year). During the time from the ninth year onwards roughly to the end of puberty the bones of the wrist solidify in their inner structure.*

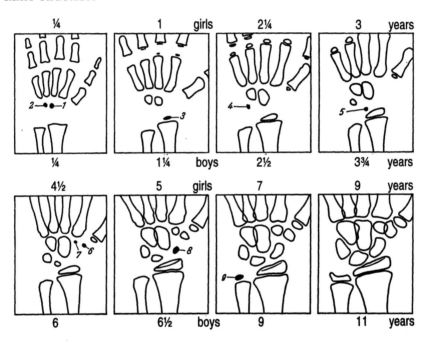

Figure 87. Development of the bones of the wrist in girls and boys (the ages given are averages). (From Harnack, Kinderheilkunde, Berlin 1972.)

Before the ninth year the scale of the ossified skeletal part of the arms sounds in a kind of fifth mood, since the fourth is not yet embodied in the skeleton. With the appearance of the last bone of the

* The sesamoid bones remain out of consideration, since they do not belong to the actual supporting skeleton of the wrist, but present rather the ossification of the tendons which pass here. We include here the epiphyses of the ulna and radius as part of the wrist.

wrist after the ninth year the qualities of the fourth become accessible to the musical consciousness. The diatonic mood develops out of the mood of the fifth. The justification of Steiner's educational indication for music making up to the ninth year in the mood of the fifth, is given by the correctly read X-ray picture.

34.8 The middle part of the hand

In the fifth a counter-stream comes from the direction of the octave. In the sixth it unfolds completely, in order in the seventh to attain greatest intensity. In this way the double origin of the human being in conception becomes audible. The mother receives out of the cosmos the individuality of the child with the spirit-seed of its head. The organs for this lie in the sphere of the fifth of her body. From the father the child receives the strength through which it builds up the remaining part of the earthly body out of the head. As adults we feel we are within this body up to the fourth. In the fifth we reach in our feeling the boundary of the body. In the intervals sixth, seventh and octave, the human being with his present-day earthly consciousness is not yet fully incarnated; this lies in the future. From this musical context of the whole human being, let us now look at the cross-section of the skeleton through the wrist, the base of the hand, the middle of the hand and the middle finger (Figure 88).

The rounded pole of the typical three-dimensional bone structure lies proximally in the collar-bone, upper arm, and ulna; the widened end lies towards the outside. In the bones of the wrist the latter sculptural stream, directed outwards from within, is constricted and cleft. In the bones of the middle hand it has been reversed. The head of the bone now lies outside, and the socket inside. All the finger-joints appear formed in this direction, from outside to inside.

The reversal of the sculptural stream occurs within the bones of the wrist itself. The one sculptural stream comes from outside into the wrist, where it is met by the sculptural stream raying out from the body in the S-formed rift in the joints of the wrist bones. In the sculptured formation of the bones of the middle hand up to the fingertips, we have the arrested picture of the musical counter-stream

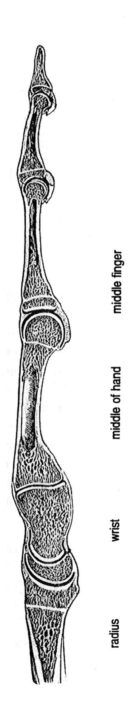

Figure 88. Longitudinal section through radius, wrist, middle of hand and middle finger (from: Toldt-Hochstetter, Anatomische Atlas).

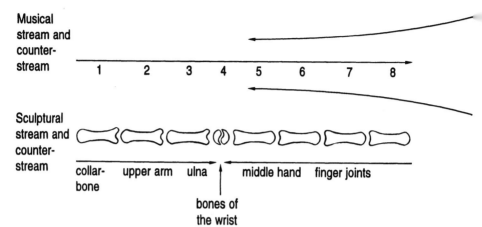

Figure 89.

before us, which streams in from the octave as far as the fifth. When it penetrates over the boundary of the fourth in the wrist as far as the radius, then experience of the minor comes about.

In order to find the direction of stream in the ulna and radius, we have to consider that nothing spherical remains where the third is active; everything is determined by invagination. Nevertheless the head-pole still remains recognizable, in that it forms that part of the bone where its main mass is concentrated.

In order to gain a correct picture of the life-body here, we have especially to take the functional movements into account which we described above with throwing and catching a ball. In the functional movement of a body part, creative action with its form in the ether body does indeed continue. In this way the following

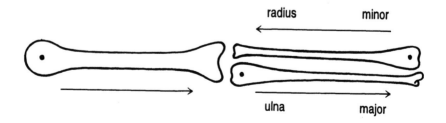

Figure 90.

picture arises from the movements of the etheric body in the lower arm (the dots mark the centre of the heads; also compare Figure 80, (page 216).

34.9 The fingers

When we unfold the fingers in accord with the movement for the sixth in eurythmy, we can feel how the muscles which spread the fingers in the sixth are situated on the lower arm. This muscular movement, streaming from within outwards, lays hold of the sculptured forms which are formed from outside inwards. The muscular system as the organization of the will spans the past and the future form and creates a unity out of both of them. Since the intervals of sixth, seventh and octave lead us to a future spiritual condition, they are physically incorporated in such small bones becoming ever more delicate. The eighth degree is the smallest, the end of the fingers. The movement for the octave in eurythmy encompasses the whole human form in its movement. Because the octave experience is still so distant, the eurythmic presentation today is only possible as an indication. Steiner's indications for showing the interval are only suggestive. When we contemplate the delicate bones indicating the octave with the means acquired from the sculptural limb exercise, then the fundamental sculpture principle of the whole human form arises.

Figure 91. The end of the finger.

35. The linguistic structure of the arm

The arm and the hand mediate between the human being and the surrounding world. The human being works physically in the world through his arms by allowing his inner nature to flow over into action, impressing the world with the stamp of his individual inner being. In language the contrast of 'I' and world appears in sentence construction as subject and object:

The farmer ploughs the field.

The basic form of the sentence — subject, verb, object — shows the function of the arm in linguistic form. It appears as the verb, through which the subject acts on the object.

Let us return to the musical level of the physiology of the arm. The hand is added to the human being from outside, from the environment. Its fifth-nature shows musically and sculpturally that the human being calls parts 'his own' which in reality are universal processes incorporated into him (the same applies to the sense organs). The will, which reaches out beyond the realm of the fourth, encroaches into universal processes, even if we consider these from the physical point of view as belonging to 'our body.' Consequently, speaking musically and sculpturally, we have to say: My experience as subject is transferred in the hand into the experience that something meets me out of the world; my consciousness as subject is penetrated with an object consciousness. 'Object' comes from the Latin *ob(j)icere,* 'to throw towards.' The grammatical object pole of the arm begins with the hand. In the shoulder-joint the arm is incorporated into the real physical form of the subject, the torso.

In this way, the archetypal form of the sentence, subject – verb – object, appears as the ego-structure of the musical anatomy of the arm.

| *Sentence* | 'The farmer | ploughs | the field' |
| | (subject | verb | object) |

| *Triad* | Keynote (2nd) | Third (fourth) | Fifth |
| for instance: | C | E | G |

Arm movement	collar-bone	ulna (wrist)	hand
in eurythmy	(upper arm)		
	shoulder-blade		

As we know in music eurythmy, the actual experience of the movement between myself and the world develops in the third; consequently the further regions of the other intervals only come into consideration with a further differentiation.

What in eurythmy is a well-known anatomical connection, is thus demonstrated in the organization of language as the basic sentence structure. This can be tested in various ways. We can feel musically the missing verb: The farmer ... the field. An empty space comes about, a vacuum, which like a fifth remains open. Life itself produces such a mood when for instance a farmer *looks* at a field in the evening which he has not been able to plough, to which no active relationship comes about because other things required his time and energy. The merely passive perception corresponds in the will to an emptiness which lies in the fifth. The difference between the subject-verb tension on the one hand and the verb-object one on the other hand produces the corresponding parallels:

The farmer ploughs ...

is the major third of a triad, for example C – E. Here an activity is present which 'rays out' from the subject in the major. On the other hand

... ploughs the field

is the minor third, E – G, which permits the passive aspect 'to suffer, or to undergo,' which predominates on the side of the object.

You see, everyone knows what a melody is; you also know what a sentence is. Few people recognize that a sentence

consisting of a subject, verb and object is really a melody in
the unconscious ... 'The child writes his essay': subject –
verb – object. A triad, a common chord, is experienced in
our innermost depths. What is felt deep down is a triad.
This triad is employed by applying the first note to the
child, the second to the writing, and the third to the essay
(Steiner[162]).

In this way we understand something of the ego-structure of the
arm in the grammatical archetype of the sentence; the arm of the soul
as the major and minor triad, and the etheric arm as sculptural stream
and counter-stream.

36 Eurythmy and musical reality

The deeper a musician or music-lover lives into the works of the great
masters, the stronger the following reservation regarding music
eurythmy can arise: The fullness of experience and the intensity of the
inner conception and form are intensified by concentrating on the
music that is heard. By withdrawing from the other senses, this
experience increases; I might even close my eyes. The deeper I lay
hold of music, the less I see either the possibility or the necessity to
follow with my eyes the musical process on stage. Is music eurythmy
then at all necessary? Do musical works benefit by becoming visible
through movement of the human body?

In the previous Parts we have built up from different sides a
musical structure of the human being. What is the reason that we
wake up refreshed in the morning when the previous day has made
possible a healthy sleep? This refreshment is the result of the activity
of the astral body during the night. As soon as it leaves the senses and
we fall asleep, it begins, in harmony with the etheric body (no longer
its antagonist) to regenerate the exhausted physical forces. It returns
to the world of the music of the spheres out of which it originates.
With the cosmic music which forms us at the embryo stage, the astral
body heals again every night that which it destroyed during the day.

Furthermore for those organs whose activity does not rise to consciousness even during the day, in which we are consequently asleep such as the liver, spleen, bone marrow, the kidneys, and so on, the astral body is active in this spiritual music during the day too. It loses contact to this world only with that part of itself with which it lives in the senses. The inner musical structure can be called a 'music held fast in the human organs.' The human being needs and requires it in order to be healthy. In the previous Parts it was repeatedly shown where the inwardly musical organization of the human being reaches a boundary at which it slips out of this condition of 'imprisonment.' The musical flow, which travels through the various organs from the activity of the feet upwards, reaches the boundary where it manifests as outer sound with exhalation in the larynx. In musical experience we conceived the seventh as this dynamic of inversion. The physiology and anatomy of the organs of the throat showed the varied activity of this interval. Eurythmy brought before our eyes how in the movements of the major and minor chords musical gestures of lung development become visible, or the function of the parathyroid glands in the gesture for the seventh.

In this sense every movement of music eurythmy is a revelation of cosmic music active in the human being. When the performing eurythmist changes into a flowing fifth or sixth, the viewer experiences what the fifth or sixth do in the human being as cosmic forces. In the particular, audible notes of the piece by Mozart which are heard in the moment and whose music is being made visible through these movements, quite specific metamorphoses resound from these cosmic sounds. They are determined by historical and personal circumstances and the conditions prevailing in the course of the piece. The composer carries the nightly sounds of the music of the spheres, which stream through his body, into the daytime in such a way as his talents and his destiny allow. In the movements of music eurythmy there appears that which is given to all human beings as the creative archetypal images of these sounds and intervals from the characteristic movements of the spiritual world. For eurythmy is an art deriving from the consciousness which the night penetrates in spiritual clarity. In this way every bar of music unfolds in its archetype through the union with the human being engaged in eurythmy.

Ever since the beginning of the twentieth century, when the creative force in the old sense expired, the consciousness soul has asked, on what reality is music based? Eurythmy is the visible answer to this question. The works of classical music, heard with the inner attitude of their age, do not need to be made visible through eurythmy. But the soul, realizing it has changed, would not be able to rediscover itself in such a transposition to an historical condition of soul. Neither would it find the contemporary relevance of this music by such means. It needs to experience that these musical works are revealed as metamorphoses of those archetypes in which the spiritual part of the human being is active at night. For working musicians the 'way of closed eyes' will remain their way in future, even when they avail themselves of 'visible singing.' They will spiritually lay hold of the characteristic movements of musical sound in order to fashion these forms for composition and performance. All human beings however behold in eurythmy the musical reality of the human being which is longed for in the depths of the soul. They behold that which in the night occurs or even wants to occur for the healing of their body.

Eurythmy came into being at about the time when the fixing of music to electro-mechanical sound producers arrived; that is, a making spatial of music in a sub-sensory sense. This development today rips the nightly deeds of spiritual beings out of the bodies of young people who visit discotheques, and attempts to push them in the direction of animality. Volume is sought in such places, in order to feel the link between music and their own physical bodies, to dream themselves into this body. Eurythmy provides the body with the musical movement which the soul knows from its body-free existence at night. The soul, which during the day leads the body into the movements of its spiritual nature, awakens to its freedom.

The study of the human being through art as the basis of anthroposophical vocational training

If we look at the position which anthroposophy currently occupies in our culture we will see first of all the Waldorf schools, the curative education institutions, anthroposophical medicine and bio-dynamic agriculture, as well as the activities of the eurythmy groups and theatre companies. And we are faced with the urgent question how the development of living anthroposophical material can keep pace with this ever-growing quantitative expansion.

One aspect of the problem is training. What significance is there for the individual in going through the training for an anthroposophical occupation? If they were familiar with anthroposophy beforehand, it was important on a personal level up to that point. Now they want to and must acquire the ability to work for other people on the basis of anthroposophy. In this situation the training has to overcome a tendency in which anthroposophy fails to progress from its previous purely personal significance and remains stuck in one way or another in the trainee's personal life. If that happens, their professional work will not advance much beyond what can be found to an equal extent outside the anthroposophical movement. The source of anthroposophical life is the path of individual schooling which is based on the study of the science of the spirit. The purpose of the abilities and the knowledge which are thus awakened is the practical implementation of anthroposophy in the life of society. Training is situated in the middle between these two poles: it is here that the facility must be acquired which enables students to transform the capacities which they develop from their study of the source material in such a way that they can be recognized as anthroposophy in the results of their practical activity. The less the training process succeeds in fulfilling this objective the more the consequences make themselves felt at both poles: personal egoism at the pole of the individual path of schooling and pragmatism as increasingly powerful influence at the other pole, in anthroposophical institutions.

On the one hand, the science of the spirit appears merely to enrich the personal life of the individual. On the other, the danger arises that anthroposophical impulses lose all significance in our occupational activity.

However, seen from a historical perspective, anthroposophy itself demonstrates how a way can be found to fertilize the life of society: through art. The climax of Rudolf Steiner's artistic activity, the first Goetheanum, became the point of entry for anthroposophy into the social conditions of that time, the buttress on which the work on the threefold social order rested. The fertilization of the individual fields — medicine, education and agriculture — began.

Thus it is not surprising that in April 1924 Steiner explains this training method, which combines three arts with science, to three different professional groups; we refer to his remarks on the use of sculpture, music and language, which he explained in detail to teachers in Stuttgart on April 10, to doctors in Dornach on April 24, and to eurythmists on April 30, 1924.[163] Many other statements on the same subject are available, including from earlier periods. The references quoted here are the most detailed. We explained the principles which underlie this way of working at the beginning of the book, and having sought to implement it throughout this study, we will examine it still from the perspective of a reform of vocational training methods.

Source:	Personal path of schooling and area of life	Danger of egoism. Anthroposophy as merely personal enrichment.
?	Training issue	Danger of pragmatic adaption to prevailing
Purpose:	Practical implementation of anthroposophy in the life of society	circumstances; danger of the loss of anthroposophical substance.

In order to understand what Rudolf Steiner is saying, all the ambiguities which have gradually come to be associated with the concept 'artistic' have to be put out of mind. His words demand from the start that everything should be abandoned which is based on a habitual, attractively comfortable relationship to traditional art. In the lectures to Waldorf teachers mentioned above, he therefore spoke of the necessity 'not to allow the artistic element to exist in our culture as a luxury alongside serious life — treating it as a luxury, even if we think of life in spiritual terms in other respects — but that we should understand it as something which penetrates the world and human beings everywhere as a law of the divine spirit.' Art in this sense sacrifices its independent existence for the service of the cognitive task of science. The artistic experience is manifest as cognitive experience. But science has to realize that without assimilating art it will never transcend death, let alone overcome it.

This method of investigating the supersensory elements of the human being starts, as we saw, where the latter reveal their surplus forces as the power which generates art. The etheric body no longer has a substrate for its sculptural impulses in the finished, fully grown physical body; in the sculptor they metamorphose into sculpture. Similarly music represents the form taken by surplus astral formative impulses which are reflected and liberated by the mature body. Language gives expression of the power which turns this physical, sculptural and musical structure into the instrument of the essential nature of human beings.

How, then, in the context of the 'training issue' does this method work in the life of an anthroposophical initiative?

On the one hand there is our inner experience and knowledge, on the other the active will. A new form of art as understood by anthroposophy turns these two direct soul impulses into the ability to act, into skill. In this skill both original impulses have overcome the personal element and can be dedicated purely to pursuing their purpose — they are united with it. But this 'purpose' is the human being himself. All the occupations which have been renewed through anthroposophy have as their aim the realization of the the true human being. That is why in the diagram below, Rudolf Steiner's answer to the training issue is represented as art-related cognitive work by the human being. It is possible to see from the diagram that this method is based on the spiritual law according to which the path of consciousness always runs counter to the path by which the spirit is creatively active; or — for those who are in the middle of training — should be active.

This work starts completely externally in the sphere to which our senses have access without our doing. And thus it starts on a cognitive level in the social circumstances of our present culture which is ready for this stage of the path. The study of language brings this method into the region which borders on the individual's meditative use of language. By means of sculpture and music we move from outside through the etheric and astral bodies into the innermost realm of the word, the 'I.' Just as the essential element lives in between the notes in music, so the Goethean approach to thinking lives in this method; an approach in which the thinking experiences the step from one element of the human being to the next by transforming itself to accord with each stage.[164]

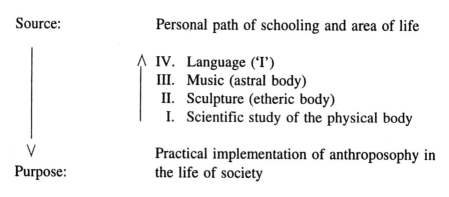

Source: Personal path of schooling and area of life

              IV. Language ('I')
             III. Music (astral body)
            II. Sculpture (etheric body)
           I. Scientific study of the physical body

Purpose: Practical implementation of anthroposophy in
                               the life of society

Anthroposophical vocational training, too, imparts learning; its primary purpose, however, is to lead its students onto a path in which they themselves become productive through the science of the spirit. The training which Rudolf Steiner set out for the fourth seven-year cycle is capable of this. For right from the beginning it does away with the dualism of theoretical classes in the science of the spirit and practical artistic exercise. It represents anthroposophy not only in its content, but as a path. That is what its students are seeking and what they need in their occupational activity.

Since speech formation, music, sculpture and eurythmy are taught at most training centres alongside the study of the human being, the only thing which is required to develop this way of working is the readiness to relate these subjects to one another. Anyone who has experienced the impact of such cooperation must ask themselves whether we can do without it in our current situation. The spiritual entities which guide our present culture expect such a way of working as laid out by Rudolf Steiner:

> As it moves to the next stage, the sculptural, pictorial
> element enters a kind of musical experience. The opposite
> happens as well, the return from the musical element to the
> sculptural and pictorial. These things are not produced
> arbitrarily by the human soul, but are connected with the
> most intimate impulses to which we are subject as a result
> of our position in the first third of the fifth post-Atlantean
> cultural epoch. They are prescribed to us, as it were, by the
> spiritual entities which guide this development.[165]

References and Notes

1   R. Steiner, *The Philosophy of Spiritual Activity: a* Philosophy of Freedom, Chapter 4 'The World as Percept,' p.43.
2   Wolfgang Schad, *Die Vorgeburtlichkeit des Menschen.*
3   R. Steiner, *Von Seelenrätseln,* p.150ff.
4   H. Kunze, 'Die Gestaltentstehung bei Pflanze und Tier,' in: *Goetheanistische Naturwissenschaft,* ed. W. Schad, Vol.1.
5   See also F.W. Zeylmans van Emmichoven, *Die menschliche Seele,* p.21ff.
6   O. Hertwig, *Das Werden der Organismen,* p.379ff.
    Th. Goebel, *Tycho de Brahe,* p.58ff.
    G. Wachsmuth, *Die ätherischen Bildekräfte im Kosmos, Erde und Mensch,* p.196.
    G. Zickwolf, 'Leben und Bewusstsein,' in: W Schad (ed), *Goetheanistische Naturwissenschaft,* Vol.1.
7   W. Schad, 'Vom Naturlaut zum Sprachlaut,' in: W Schad (ed), *Goetheanistische Naturwissenschaft,* Vol.1, p.90ff.
8   R. Steiner, *Meditative Betrachtungen und Anleitungen zur Vertiefung der Heilkunst,* evening meeting on April 24, 1924. See also the lecture of April 25, 1924.
9   R. Steiner, *Allgemeine Menschenkunde,* lecture of September 1, 1919.
10 C.H. Stratz, *Der Körper des Kindes und seine Pflege,* Stratz's indications are not based on his own scientific research. They rely on measurements taken by:
    Richer, *Canon des Proportions du corps humain,* 1893;
    Otto Geyer, *Der Mensch, Hand- und Lehrbuch,* 1902;
    Gottfried Schadow, *Polyklet,* 1834;
    Monti, *Kinderheilkunde in Einzeldarstellung,* Vienna 1899.
    Stratz was still in the tradition of those scientists who distinguished between an ideal standard measurement and statistical average values. But the Figure which is reproduced here accords near enough with more recent research by Medawar, Scammon, Calkins and our own measurements, so that the proportions and ages can be taken as sufficiently accurate to serve as mean values. The following measurements were taken from newborns and children by Dr Godhard Husemann, for which I would like to take this opportunity to thank him. The adult measurements were made by the author.

Size of group	Age group	Average head height	Values given by Stratz
32	4–12 weeks	4.5	4 (newborn)
18	5.0–7.4 years	5.92	6 (age 6)
10	11.4–13.4 yrs	7.19	7 (age 12)
23	20–61 years	8.19	8 (age 24)

P.B. Medawar, 'Size shape and age,' in: *Essays on growth and form*, ed. by W.E. Le Gros Clar and P.B. Medawar.
R.E. Scammon, H.A. Calkins, *Development and Growth of the Human Body*.

11   Quételet quoting C.H. Stratz, *Der Körper des Kindes und seine Pflege;* also quoted by Prof. G. Gupka in his inaugural lecture in Tübingen on assuming the chair of child endocrinology, 1977.

12   R. Steiner, *Erziehung und Unterricht aus Menschenerkenntnis*, lecture of September 22, 1920.

13   R. Steiner, *Das Sonnenmysterium*, lecture of April 1, 1922.

14   R. Steiner, *Die Entstehung und Entwicklung der Eurythmie*, p.74ff. (August 24, 1915).

15   G.W.F. Hegel, *Enzyklopädie der philosophischen Wissenschaften*, Part II, p.452.

16   R. Steiner, question and answer session of September 30, 1920 in: *Das Wesen des Musikalischen und das Tonerleben im Menschen.*

17   R. Steiner, *Die Methodik des Lehrens*, lecture of April 10, 1924.

18   R. Steiner, *Die Geheimwissenschaft im Umriss*, p.288.

19   W. Marget, 'Infektionskrankheiten,' in: W. Keller, A. Wiskott, *Lehrbuch der Kinderheilkunde.*

20   R. Steiner, *Perspektiven der Menschheitsentwicklung*, lecture of April 23, 1921.

21   The proportions between numbers, say 4/5, can be made to sound in a number of ways on the monochord. The first thing which must be remembered is that the frequency (number of vibrations per second, Hz) is in inverse proportion to the length of the string. The greater the length of the vibrating string, the less the frequency and the lower the tone. This inverse relationship is expressed such that the proportion between two lengths of string (for instance 4/5) corresponds in inverse proportion to the frequency (5/4). The first way in which a proportion such as 4/5 can be made to sound is by dividing the string into nine sections; one can do that by placing a strip of paper under the string and then marking nine divisions. Then one need only count off four sections from one side and place a movable bridge at that spot. Five sections will remain on the other part of the string. If one then uses a bow on both sections the proportions 4/9 and 5/9 will sound. Since the common denominator does not have any bearing on the ratio, we thus hear 4:5. But only if we first make the 4/9

of the left part (in Figure 25) sound and then the right part. If we first make the right part of the string sound (5/9) and then the left (4/9) then we hear 5:4. The interval remains the same, but the motion changes direction.

Let us still deal with a second method, although it is in fact a natural consequence of the one explained above, because it is the one which is used in the first part. 5/4 can also be made to sound by dividing the string into 4/4 and 5/5 (on the paper). Then 1/4 can be made to sound. Thereafter the bridge can be moved to the spot where 1/5 is marked. In that way, too, 5/4 sounds, because 1/4:1/5 = 5/4. It will be immediately clear why it was necessary to use this process in the first part if we take the overall length of the shape in Figure 6 as the length of the string and always divide it where the head size in each shape ends at the chin. In this way the intervals resulted from the ratio of two different points of time. The stage at which the embryo has a head size of 1/3 of the total changes in time into one where it is only 1/4 of the overall length. If the bridge of the monochord is moved from 1/3 to 1/4 then the ratio of these two fractions sounds as 1/3:1/4 = 4/3 or a frequency of 3/4. Thus the first method can be used to make spatial proportions sound whereas the second one will represent changes over time.

We need to refer to one further case and that is when we want to produce a sound ratio which includes the number 1, for instance 1:3, 1/3, or, as on page 163, 1:24. Then the sound made by one third of the string has to be brought into relationship with the whole string. The one tone is the undivided string (= 1), the other is the string shortened to 1/3. A detailed explanation of the monochord, as well as instructions on how to build one, can be found in the book by H. Ruland, *Ein Weg zur Erweiterung des Tonerlebens.*

22 R. Steiner, *Das Wesen des Musikalischen,* lecture of March 8, 1923.

23 R. Steiner, *Das Wesen des Musikalischen,* GA 283, lecture of November 12, 1906.

24 I am indebted for this thought to Maria Schüppel, head of Musiktherapeutische Arbeitsstätte [Centre for Music Therapy] in Berlin. Of course the melodic sequence of the lengthening string has to be taken into account as well. We cannot go into that here, however, since this would open up a whole new field.

25 The arrows indicate that these notes — we are here in an untempered system — change slightly in the direction of the arrows. The sound in 7 is a slightly smaller minor third while the sound in 8 is a slightly larger second.

26 Eight public lectures from August 29 to September 6, 1921, published in German as *Anthroposophie, ihre Erkenntniswurzeln und Lebensfrüchte,* and in English as *The Fruits of Anthroposophy.*

27 R. Steiner, in: *Goethes naturwissenschaftliche Schriften,* Vol.1, p. xxxiii.

28 E. Haeckel, *Kunstformen der Natur,* and *Wanderbilder nach eigenen*

Aquarellen und Ölgemälden, Serie I & II: 'Naturwunder der Tropenwelt Ceylon und Insulinde.'

29   E. Meffert, *Carl Gustav Carus.*

30   R. Steiner, *Anthroposophie, ihre Erkenntniswurzeln und Lebensfrüchte*, lecture of September 2, 1921.

31   Grosser-Ortmann, *Grundriß der Entwicklungsgeschichte der Menschen*, p.49ff;
K.L. Moore, *Embryologie*, p.63.

32   E. Haeckel, *Studien zur Gastraea-Theorie*, Jena 1877.

33   E. Haeckel, *Anthropogenie*, Vol.1, p.160.

34   E. Haeckel, *Anthropogenie*, Vol.1, p.175.

35   In this sense Carus described the animal as a 'hollow invaginated sphere filled with entrails' (*Von den Naturreichen* [1818]). Quoted from Meffert, *Carl Gustav Carus.*

36   This was his *Welt- und Lebensanschauungen des 19. Jahrhunderts* later (1914) expanded into *Die Rätsel der Philosophie.*

37   R. Steiner, *Anthroposophie, ihre Erkenntniswurzeln und Lebensfrüchte*, lecture of September 2, 1921.

38   R. Steiner, *Anthroposophie, ihre Erkenntniswurzeln und Lebensfrüchte*, lecture of September 2, 1921.

39   R. Steiner, *Das Geheimnis der Trinität*, lecture of July 28, 1922.

40   C. Elze, in: Braus-Elze, *Anatomie des Menschen*, Vol.3, p.457 and 470.

41   C. Elze, in: Braus-Elze, *Anatomie des Menschen*, Vol.3, p.566.

42   H. Braus, in: Braus-Elze, *Anatomie des Menschen*, Vol.1, p.692.

43   D. Starck, *Vergleichende Anatomie der Wirbeltiere*, Vol.3, p.396.

44   G. Husemann, 'Der Liquor cerebro-spinalis,' in: *Beiträge zu einer Erweiterung der Heilkunst*, 1980 nos. 1 and 4, 1983 No. 3.

45   R. Steiner, *Meditative Betrachtungen zur Vertiefung der Heilkunst*, evening meeting of April 24, 1924.

46   R. Steiner, *Allgemeine Menschenkunde*, lecture of September 5, 1919.

47   R. Steiner, *Fruits of Anthroposophy*, lecture of September 2, 1921.

48   R. Steiner, *Grundlegendes für eine Erweiterung der Heilkunst*, Chapter 1.

49   For the dynamic qualities of the intervals compare for example Zuckerkandl, *Die Wirklichkeit der Musik*, p.94ff. The attempt to 'fix' the qualities of intervals is frequently rejected. Thus Jürgen Uhde, for example, writes in the otherwise outstanding work *Beethovens Klaviermusik*, Vol.1, p.422: 'An interval can change its character a great deal! The attempt to define the nature of intervals in terms of their character must remain fruitless.' This is only true for as long as one fails to grasp qualities like those of intervals with the relevant cognitive flexibility. Without Goethe's way of thinking, aesthetics in particular will fail to penetrate the life of works of art. The interval (or any other musical quality) can be understood as an archetype which contains a wealth of metamorphoses as the 'repertoire' of its manifestations. It is also often misunderstood that the archetype of the quality of an interval can appear in a completely alien setting; for example,

if other musical processes such as a rhythmic or harmonic event were more important to the composer at a particular point than the melodic interval. After all, in general a great variety of determinants and relationships overlap and penetrate one another in a note or interval. If one seeks out the places where one quality dominates (examples 1-3) then these largely accord with one another within the relevant stylistic musical period.

50   R. Steiner, postscript in: W. Blume, *Musikalische Betrachtungen.*

51   The same principle underlies the nervous substance, which is subject to death because of this separation of the etheric body from the physical body. Ideas become conscious in the nervous system (brain) in so far as they are tied to sensory perceptions. The generative activity which prevails as the creative life of ideas, both in objects and in the thinking, comes to consciousness in the cerebrospinal fluid.

52   D. Starck, *Vergleichende Anatomie der Wirbeltiere,* Vol.3, p.396.

53   R. Steiner, *Die Geheimwissenschaft im Umriss,* chapter: 'Die Weltentwicklung und der Mensch.'

54   R. Steiner, *Grundlinien einer Erkenntnistheorie,* pp.103, 107f.

55   R. Steiner, *Allgemeine Menschenkunde,* lecture of September 4, 1919.

56   R. Steiner, 'Der· geniale Mensch,' in: *Methodische Grundlagen der Anthroposophie,* p.422-432.

57   R. Steiner, *Aus der Akasha-Chronik,* p.75.

58   R. Steiner, *Aus der Akasha-Chronik,* p.77.

59   R. Steiner, *Das Johannes-Evangelium,* lecture of May 31, 1908.

60   R. Steiner, in: *Goethes naturwissenschaftliche Schriften,* Vol.2, p.iv.

61   R. Steiner, *Die Philosophie der Freiheit,* p.143.

62   *Welt- und Lebensanschauungen des 19. Jahrhunderts* appeared in 1900/ 1901 and in an expanded new edition in 1914 as *Rätsel der Philosophie.*

63   R. Steiner, *Die Rätsel der Philosophie,* p.403.

64   R. Steiner, *Mein Lebensgang,* p.402f.

65   R. Steiner, *Die Geheimwissenschaft,* p.174.

66   R. Steiner and Marie Steiner-von Sivers, *Correspondence and Documents,* p.13.

67   R. Steiner, *Mysterienstätten des Mittelalters,* lecture of January 13, 1924.

68   E. Kolisko, *Auf der Suche nach neuen Wahrheiten,* 'Die zwölf Gruppen des Tierreiches' (p.124ff). R. Steiner, *Konferenzen mit den Lehrern,* (Vol.3) meeting of April 25, 1923.

69   R. Steiner, in: *Goethes naturwissenschaftliche Schriften,* Vol.1, p. lxxi.

70   R. Steiner, *Philosophie der Freiheit,* p.200.

71   F. Hollwich, *Augenheilkunde,* p.3.

72   Compare R. Steiner, *Die Philosophie der Freiheit,* GA 4, Chapter 9.

73   R. Steiner, *Eurythmie als sichtbarer Gesang,* GA 278, Dornach 3 ed 1975, lecture of February 21, 1924. Also in English as: *Eurythmy as Visible Song,* R. Steiner Press, London 1977.

74   Benninghoff-Goerttler, *Lehrbuch der Anatomie,* Vol.2, p.280: 'The nucleus (of the sperm) consists of condensed chromatin which is extremely stable·

in relation to chemical and physical influences ... During spermiogenesis finely distributed chromatin elements condense into larger particles ...' The sperm cell is the only point in the organism where observation of the single cell as a self-contained whole is justified. For it is as a single cell that it produces the whole human being with fertilization of the female egg cell. The same applies to the latter. No other cell in the body should be observed in this way as a self-contained whole.

75   G. Suchantke, E. Pracht, 'Quart und Quint im Menschen,' *Natura* 1927/28 (Vol.2), p.364ff.

76   R. Steiner, 'Das Tonerlebnis im Menschen,' in: *Das Wesen des Musikalischen,* lecture of March 7, 1923.

77   Benninghoff-Goerttler, *Lehrbuch der Anatomie,* Vol.1, p.271.

78   Benninghoff-Goerttler, *Lehrbuch der Anatomie,* Vol.1, p.368.

79   R. Steiner, 'Das Tonelerbnis im Menschen,' in: *Das Wesen des Musikalischen,* lecture of March 7, 1923.

80   R. Steiner, *Grundlegendes zu einer Erweiterung der Heilkunst,* Chapter 14.

81   F. Kuhlencordt, et al, *Lehrbuch der Inneren Medizin,* p.725ff.

82   G. Seifert in: M. Eder, P. Gedik, *Lehrbuch der allgemeinen Pathologie,* p.566.

83   S. Jenny in: R. Heggelin, *Differentialdiagnose innerer Krankheiten,* p.189.

84   F.S. Brodnitz, 'Sänger und Schauspieler als Patienten des Laryngologen' in: *Hals- Nasen-Ohren-Heilkunde in Klinik und Praxis,* ed. by J. Berendes, et al, Vol.4, Part 1.

85   R. Steiner, *Heileurythmiekurs,* lecture of April 12, 1921.

86   R. Steiner, *Eurythmie als sichtbarer Gesang,* lecture of February 20, 1924.

87   R. Steiner, a) *Geisteswissenschaftliche Gesichtspunkte zur Therapie,* lecture of April 12, 1921; b) *Geisteswissenschaftliche Impulse zur Entwicklung der Physik,* lectures of March 13 and 14, 1920; c) *Grundelemente der Esoterik,* lecture of September 30, 1905.

88   R. Steiner, notebook entries for the music eurythmy course lectures. Supplement to *Eurythmie als sichtbarer Gesang,* notebook entry for the lecture of February 21, 1924.

89   R. Steiner, *Eurythmie als sichtbarer Gesang,* lecture of February 21, 1924.

90   M. Simon jr., 'Diagnostische Hauptsymptome bei Hyper- und Hypothyreose,' in: *Therapiewoche,* Vol.37, No. 46 of November 16, 1987.

91   H. Bickel, et al, *Lehrbuch der Kinderheilkunde,* p.14.79.

92   R. Steiner, *Grundlegendes für eine Erweiterung der Heilkunst,* Chapter 5.

93   H. Bickel, et al, *Lehrbuch der Kinderheilkunde,* p.15.28.

94   F. Kuhlencordt, et al, *Lehrbuch der Inneren Medizin,* p.736.

95   R. Steiner, Notes Nos. 820-822, in: Goethe, *Sprüche in Prosa,* p.164.

96   R. Steiner, *Das Wesen des Musikalischen,* lecture of December 3, 1906.

97   R. Steiner, 'Okkulte Zeichen und Symbole,' lecture of December 29, 1907, in: *Mythen und Sagen. Okkulte Zeichen und Symbole.*

98   F. Kuhlencordt, et al, *Lehrbuch der Inneren Medizin,* p.942, and D. Starck, *Vergleichende Anatomie der Wirbeltiere,* Vol.3, p.689.

99   J.F. Habener, J.T. Pott jr., 'Chemistry, biosynthesis and metabolism of parathyroid hormone,' in: *Handbook of physiology,* Vol.7, p.315, American Physiological Society, Washington DC, 1976.

100 R. Steiner in: W. Blume, *Musikalische Betrachtungen,* p.33.

101 R. Steiner, *Meditative Betrachtungen,* evening meeting of April 24, 1924.

102 R. Steiner, *Weltenwunder, Seelenprüfungen und Geistesoffenbarungen,* third lecture of August 20, 1911.

103 J. W. von Goethe, *Tag- und Jahreshefte,* Vol.10, p.436.

104 R. Steiner, *Meditative Betrachtungen,* sixth lecture of January 7, 1924.

105 R. Steiner, *Aus der Akasha-Chronik,* chapter 'Die letzten Zeiten vor der Geschlechtertrennung' [The last period before the division into the sexes].

106 E. Dondelinger, *Der Obelisk.*

107 '... if one can manage ... to place before the inner eye this internal part of thinking and an element of the feeling, then one has ... something which belongs together with what the embryologist finds in embryonic development and, indeed, in cell development in general. One can see the following if one compares the original manifestation and its reflection: on the one hand there is the thinking and feeling process in the soul and on the other the process of fertilization, the process of nuclear division and so on — of cell division itself. One can see ... how the one, translated into matter, represents what the other is in the soul and spiritual field.' (R. Steiner, 'Anthroposophie und Naturwissenschaft' in: *Die Ergänzung heutiger Wissenschaft durch Anthroposophie,* third lecture of November 12, 1917.)

108 This section reproduces in expanded form material which Gisbert Husemann presented at the course on the study of the human being from a sculptural, musical and language perspective in Stuttgart in 1975.

109 R. Steiner, *Kunst und Kunsterkenntnis,* two lectures of February 15 and 17, 1918.

110 I owe the song of the Hopi Indians to Heiner Ruland (Conference for music therapists, Filderstadt 1985), and the Mongolian lullaby to Felix Lindenmaier (Working week for the study of the human being through art, Dornach 1986).

111 H. Ruland, 'Quint und Terz als musikalische und musiktherapeutische Agentien' in: *Beiträge zu einer Erweiterung der Heilkunst,* 1982, No. 2.

112 G. Husemann, lectures in the Working week for the study of the human being through art, Stuttgart 1977.

113 F. Husemann, 'Das Belladonnagift und seine Wirkprinzipien,' *Beiträge zur Erweiterung der Heilkunst,* 1979, No. 6.

114 R. Steiner, *Der Mensch als Zusammenklang des schaffenden, bildenden und gestaltenden Weltenwortes.*

115 In his book *Säugetiere und Mensch,* W. Schad develops the concept of threefold division in relation to the mammals, which he classifies as a result into rodents, beasts of prey and hoofed animals.

116   R. Steiner, *Perspektiven der Menschheitsentwicklung,* eighth lecture of April 23, 1921.

117   R. Steiner, 'Okkulte Zeichen und Symbole' in: *Mythen und Sagen. Okkulte Zeichen und Symbole,* eighth lecture of December 29, 1907.

118   'Erfahrung und Wissenschaft,' essay in *Goethes Naturwissenschaftliche Schriften,* Vol.4, Section 2, p.593.

119   R. Steiner, 'Das menschliche Leben vom Gesichtspunkt der Geistes-wissenschaft (Anthroposophie)' in: *Philosophie und Anthroposophie,* p.238.

120   R. Steiner, *Esoterische Betrachtungen karmischer Zusammenhänge,* Vol.2, eighth lecture of May 10, 1924.

121   R. Steiner, *Das Sonnenmysterium,* lecture of April 1, 1922.

122   R. Steiner, 'Das Tonerlebnis im Menschen' in: *Das Wesen des Musikalischen,* third lecture of March 16, 1923.

123   R. Steiner, *Die Entstehung und Entwicklung der Eurythmie,* meeting of April 30, 1924.

124   V. Sill, et al, *Lunge und kleiner Kreislauf.*

125   H. Herzog, 'Erkrankungen der Lunge und der Pleura' in: R. Gross, P. Schölmerich, *Lehrbuch der Inneren Medizin.*

126   Harrison, *Prinzipien der Inneren Medizin,* p.1699.

127   J.B. West, 'Relationships in Ventilation-Profusion, in: J.G. Scadding (ed), *Scientific Foundations of Respiratory Medicine,* p.150.

128   P. Harris, D. Heath (ed), *The Human Pulmonary Circulation,* p.569.

129   R. Steiner, 'Das Tonerlebnis im Menschen' in: *Das Wesen des Musikalischen,* first lecture of March 7, 1923.

130   H. Lauboeck, 'Zur Beziehung zwischen der Blutkreislaufbewegung und der Herzbewegung' in: *Der Merkurstab* 3/1989, pp.125-142. This study provides outstanding evidence, by the methods of natural science, for R. Steiner's theory of the heart as damming organ and proves the absurdity of the pump concept.

131   Examples from music literature: see H. Pfrogner, *Lebendige Tonwelt,* Chapter 'musica humana.'

132   R. Steiner, *Das Wesen des Musikalischen,* first lecture of December 3, 1906.

133   R. Steiner, *Die Methodik des Lehrens,* third lecture in the morning of April 10, 1924.

134   J. Broman, *Die Entwicklung des Menschen vor der Geburt,* p.120.

135   H. Braus, *Anatomie des Menschen,* Vol.2, p.165ff; M. Hertl, *Päliatrische Differentialdiagnose,* p.56ff.

136   H. Hoepke, A. Landsberger, *Das Muskelspiel des Menschen,* p.9.

137   R. Steiner, *Die Entstehung und Entwicklung der Eurythmie,* meeting of April 30, 1924.

138   R. Steiner, *Die geistige Führung,* p.29f.

139   Revised version of the author's essay 'Tonheileurythmie aus musikalischer Menschenkunde,' in *Erziehen und Heilen durch Musik,* (Gerhard Beilharz, Stuttgart 1989).

140 R. Steiner, *Die Erneuerung der pädagogisch didaktischen Kunst,* lecture 11 (May 6, 1920).

141 R. Steiner, *Die Entstehung und Entwicklung der Eurythmie,* p.75.

142 R. Steiner, *Eurythmie als sichtbarer Gesang.*

143 G. Suchantke and E. Pracht were the first to point out the relationship between biceps and triceps and the right and left lung: 'Quint und Quart im Menschen,' *Natura* 1927/28, pp.364-375, reprint Arlesheim (Switzerland) 1981.

144 R. Steiner, *Eurythmie als sichtbare Sprache,* lecture 1 (June 24, 1924).

145 R. Steiner, *Eurythmie als sichtbarer Gesang,* lecture of February 26, 1924.

146 R. Steiner, *Eurythmie als sichtbarer Gesang,* lecture of February 27, 1924.

147 R. Steiner, *Eurythmie als sichtbarer Gesang,* lecture of February 21, 1924.

148 Steiner, *Pastoral-Medizinischer Kurs,* lecture 2, September 9, 1924.

149 R. Steiner, *Eurythmie als sichtbarer Gesang,* lecture of February 26, 1924.

150 R. Fick, *Handbuch der Anatomie der Gelenke,* Vol.3, p.207.

151 H. Braus, *Anatomie des Menschen,* Vol.2, p.153.

152 Angela Husemann, Exercises in projective geometry on the heart, in Working week for the study of the human being through art, 1980 and 1981.

153 R. Steiner, *Eurythmie als sichtbarer Gesang,* lecture of February 26, 1924.

154 G. Husemann, Working week for the study of the human being through art, Stuttgart 1973 and 1980.

155 R. Fick, *Handbuch der Anatomie der Gelenke,* Vol.3.

156 M. Woernle, 'Grundzüge der menschlichen Knochenbildung,' in: *Goethe-anistische Naturwissenschaft,* W. Schad (ed), Vol.4.

157 Report by the author on the conference on human biology through art in 1980, with Giesbert Husemann together with Reimar von Bonin, Maria Schüppel and Wilfried Hammacher contributing to the subject. Reprinted from *Beiträge zur Erweiterung der Heilkunst* 1980, No. 3.

158 G. Cruetz, *Geheimnisse des Vogelzuges,* p.63.

159 Translation from *The Penguin Book of German Verse,* ed. Leonard Forster.

160 E. Pracht, 'Die Entwicklung des Musikerlebens in der Kindheit, vom Wesen seelenpflegebedürftiger Kinder,' in: *Heilende Erziehung,* Verlag Freies Geistesleben, Stuttgart 1981, p.311.

161 P.-M. Riehm, 'Musikunterricht aus lebendiger Menschenkunde,' in: G. Beilharz (ed), *Erziehen durch Heilen und Musik,* Stuttgart 1989, p.64-92.

162 R. Steiner, *Die Erneuerung der pädagogisch-didaktischen Kunst durch Geisteswissenschaft,* lecture 2 of May 6, 1920.

163 Steiner spoke to teachers in *The Essentials of Education,* to doctors in *Meditative Betrachtungen,* and to eurythmists in *Die Entstehung und Entwicklung der Eurythmy.*

164 N. Ruff, 'Die Bedeutung der Plastisch-musikalisch-sprachlichen Menschenkunde für die Ausbildung des Architekten' in: *Beiträge zu einer Erweiterung der Heilkunst,* 1986/5, p.176ff.

165 R. Steiner, *Kunst im Lichte der Mysterienweisheit,* lecture of December 28, 1914.

Bibliography

Allgöwer, M., *Allgemeine und spezielle Chirurgie,* 3 ed, Berlin 1976.

Beilharz, G. (ed), *Erziehen durch Heilen und Musik,* Stuttgart 1989, p.64-92.

Benninghoff-Goerttler, *Lehrbuch der Anatomie des Menschen,* Urban und Schwarzenberg, Munich 9 ed 1971.

Berendes, J., R. Link and F. Zöllner (eds), *Hals-Nasen-Ohren-Heilkunde in Klinik und Praxis,* Thieme Verlag, Stuttgart 2 ed 1982.

Bickel, H., H.-J. Bremer in: W. Keller, A. Wiskott, *Lehrbuch der Kinderheilkunde,* Thieme Verlag, Stuttgart 4 ed 1977.

Blume, W., *Musikalische Betrachtungen in geisteswissenschaftlichem Sinn,* A. Husemann (ed), Dornach 2 ed 1985.

Brans, H., *Lehrbuch der Anatomie,* Vol.3.

Braus-Elze, *Anatomie des Menschen,* Vol.1, Springer, Berlin 3 ed 1954.

——, ——, Vol.2, Springer, Heidelberg 3 ed 1956.

——, ——, Vol.3, Springer, Berlin 2 ed 1960.

Broman, J., *Die Entwicklung des Menschen vor der Geburt,* Munich 1927.

Cruetz, G., *Geheimnisse des Vogelzuges,* Brehm-Bücherie, Wittenberg 8 ed 1983.

Dondelinger, E., *Der Obelisk,* Graz 1977.

Eder, M., P. Gedik, *Lehrbuch der allgemeinen Pathologie und der Pathologischen Anatomie,* Springer Verlag, Heidelberg 1975.

Elder, Duke, *System of Ophthalmology,* Vol.3.

Fick, R., *Handbuch der Anatomie der Gelenke,* Jena 1911.

Forster, Leonard (ed), *The Penguin Book of German Verse,* London 1957.

Geyer, Otto, *Der Mensch, Hand- und Lehrbuch,* 1902.

Goebel, Th., *Tycho de Brahe: Jahrbuch für Goetheanismus,* Verlag Freies Geistesleben, Stuttgart 1984.

Goethe, J.W. von, *Naturwissenschaftliche Schriften,*

——, *Sprüche in Prosa,* Freies Geistesleben, Stuttgart 1967.

——, *Tag- und Jahreshefte,* Hamburger Ausgabe, Vol.10.

Gross, R., and P. Schölmerich, *Lehrbuch der Inneren Medizin,* Schattauer Verlag, Stuttgart 1977.

Grosser-Ortmann, *Grundriß der Entwicklungsgeschichte der Menschen,* 1970.

Haeckel, E., *Anthropogenie,* 4 ed 1891.

Haeckel, E., *Kunstformen der Natur,* Leipzig 1899.

Haeckel, E., *Studien zur Gastraea-Theorie,* Jena 1877.

Haeckel, E., *Wanderbilder nach eigenen Aquarellen und Ölgemälden,* Jena 1904.

Harnack, G.A. von, *Kinderheilkunde,* Berlin 1972.

Harris, P., D. Heath (ed), *The Human Pulmonary Circulation,* Edinburgh 1986.

Harrison, *Prinzipien der Inneren Medizin,* Basel 1986.

Hegel, G.W.F., *Enzyklopädie der philosophischen Wissenschaften,* Part II, Suhrkamp Verlag, Frankfurt 1970, Vol.9 of *Werke.*

Heggelin, R., *Differentialdiagnose innerer Krankheiten,* Thieme Verlag, Stuttgart 1975.

Hertl, M., *Paediatrische Differentialdiagnose,* Thieme Verlag, Stuttgart 1977.

Hertwig, O., *Das Werden der Organismen,* 2 ed 1918.

Hoepke, H., A. Landsberger, *Das Muskelspiel des Menschen,* Gustav Fischer Verlag, Stuttgart 1979.

Hollwich, F., *Augenheilkunde,* Thieme Verlag, Stuttgart 8 ed 1976.

Keller, W., A. Wiskott, *Lehrbuch der Kinderheilkunde,* Thieme Verlag, Stuttgart 4 ed 1977.

Kolisko, E., *Auf der Suche nach neuen Wahrheiten,* Dornach 1989.

Kuhlencordt, F., H.P. Kruse in: R. Gross, P. Schölmerich, *Lehrbuch der Inneren Medizin,* Schattauer Verlag, Stuttgart, New York 1977.

Langman, *Medizinische Embryologie,* 3 ed.

Le Gros Clar, W.E. and P.B. Medawar (eds), *Essays on growth and form,* Clarendon Press, Oxford 1945.

Meffert, E., *Carl Gustav Carus, Sein Leben, seine Anschauung von der Erde,* Verlag Freies Geistesleben, Stuttgart 1986.

Monti, *Kinderheilkunde in Einzeldarstellung,* Vienna 1899.

Moore, K.L., *Embryologie,* Stuttgart 2 ed 1985.

Pfrogner, H., *Lebendige Tonwelt,* Munich 1976.

Richer, *Canon des Proportions du corps humain,* Delagrave 1893.

Ruland, H., *Ein Weg zur Erweiterung des Tonerlebens — Musikalische Tonkunde am Monochord,* Verlag Die Pforte, Basel 1981.

Scadding, J.G., *Scientific Foundations of Respiratory Medicine,* London 1981.

Scammon, R.E., H.A. Calkins, *Development and Growth of the External Dimensions of the Human Body in the Fetal Period,* University of Minnesota Press, Minneapolis 1929.

Schad, Wolfgang, *Säugetiere und Mensch,* Verlag Freies Geistesleben, Stuttgart 1971.

——, *Die Vorgeburtlichkeit des Menschen,* Verlag Urachhaus, Stuttgart 1982.

——, (ed), *Goetheanistische Naturwissenschaft,* Vol.1: *Allgemeine Biologie,* Verlag Freies Geistesleben, Stuttgart 1982.

——, ——, Vol.4, Verlag Freies Geistesleben, Stuttgart 1985.

Schadow, Gottfried, *Polyklet oder von den Massen des Menschen nach Geschlecht und Alter,* 1834.

Sill, V., E. Kaukal, K. Lauser, N. Vlkel, *Lunge und kleiner Kreislauf,* Kurzmonographie No. 22, Sandoz, 1978.

Starck, D., *Vergleichende Anatomie der Wirbeltiere,* Vol.2, Springer Velag, Berlin 1979.

——, ——, Vol.3, Springer Velag, Berlin 1982.

Steiner, *Allgemeine Menschenkunde,* Gesamtausgabe (GA) [Complete works] 293, Dornach 8 ed 1980. Also in English as: *Study of Man, General Education Course.*

——, *Anthroposophie, ihre Erkenntniswurzeln und Lebensfrüchte,* GA 78, Dornach 3 ed 1968. Also in English as: *Fruits of Anthroposophy.*

——, *Art as Seen in the Light of Mystery Wisdom,* Steiner Press, London 1984.

——, *Aus der Akasha-Chronik,* GA 11, Dornach 4 ed 1969. Also in English as: *Cosmic Memory.*

——, *Balance in Teaching,* Mercury Press, Spring Valley, NY, 1990.

——, *The Case for Anthroposophy,* Steiner Press, London 1970.

——, *Cosmic Memory,* Garber Communications, Blauvelt NY 1985.

——, *The Course of My Life,* Anthroposophic Press, New York 1986.

——, *Curative Eurythmy,* Steiner Press, London 1983.

——, *Die Entstehung und Entwicklung der Eurythmie,* GA 277a, Dornach 1965.

——, *Die Ergänzung heutiger Wissenschaft durch Anthroposophie,* GA 73, Dornach 1973.

——, *Die Erneuerung der pädagogisch-didaktischen Kunst durch Geisteswissenschaft,* GA 301, Dornach 1977. Also in English as: *The Renewal of Education.*

——, *Egyptian Myths and Mysteries,* Anthroposophic Press, New York 1971.

——, *Erziehung und Unterricht aus Menschenerkenntnis,* GA 302a, Dornach 1972. Also in English as: *Balance in Teaching.*

——, *Esoterische Betrachtungen karmischer Zusammenhänge,* Vol.2, GA 236, Dornach 1973. Also in English as: *Karmic Relationships.*

——, *The Essentials of Education,* Steiner Press, London 1982.

——, *Eurythmie als sichtbare Sprache,* GA 279, Dornach 3 ed 1968. Also in English as: *Eurythmy as Visible Speech.*

——, *Eurythmie als sichtbarer Gesang,* GA 278, Dornach 3 ed 1975. Also in English as: *Eurythmy as Visible Music.*

——, *Eurythmy as Visible Music,* Steiner Press, London 1977.

——, *Eurythmy as Visible Speech,* Steiner Press, London 1984.

——, *The Fruits of Anthroposophy,* Steiner Press, London 1986.

——, *Fundamentals of Therapy,* Steiner Press, London 1983.

——, *Das Geheimnis der Trinität,* GA 214, Dornach 2 ed 1980.

——, *Die Geheimwissenschaft im Umriss,* GA 13, Dornach 29 ed 1977. Also in English as: *Occult Science.*

——, *Geisteswissenschaftliche Gesichtspunkte zur Therapie,* GA 313, Dornach 3 ed 1963.

——, *Geisteswissenschaftliche Impulse zur Entwicklung der Physik,* (second natural science course) GA 321, Dornach 2 ed 1972. Also in English as: *Heat, the Second Scientific Lecture Course.*

——, *Die geistige Führung des Menschen und der Menschheit,* GA 15, Dornach 9 ed 1974. Also in English as: *The Spiritual Guidance of Man and Humanity.*

——, *Goethe the Scientist,* Anthroposophic press, New York 1950.

——, *Goethes naturwissenschaftliche Schriften,* GA 1, Dornach 2 ed 1975. Steiner's introduction also in English as: *Goethe the Scientist.*

——, *The Gospel of St John,* Anthroposophic Press, New York 1984.

——, *Grundelemente der Esoterik,* GA 93a, Dornach 1972. Also in English as *Rudiments of Esotericism.*

——, *Grundlegendes für eine Erweiterung der Heilkunst nach geisteswissenschaftlichen Erkenntnissen*, GA 27. Also in English as: *Fundamentals of Therapy*.

——, *Grundlinien einer Erkenntnistheorie*, GA 2. Also in English as: *A Theory of Knowledge*.

——, *Heat, the Second Scientific Lecture Course*, Mercury Press, New York.

——, *Heileurythmiekurs*, GA 315. Also in English as: *Curative Eurythmy*.

——, *The Inner Nature of Music and the Experience of Tone*, Anthroposophic Press, New York 1983.

——, *Das Johannes-Evangelium*, GA 103, Dornach 10 ed 1981. Also in English as: *The Gospel of St John*.

——, *Karmic Relationships*, Vol.2, Steiner Press, London 1974.

——, *Konferenzen mit den Lehrern der Freien Waldorfschule*, GA 300, Vol.3, Dornach 1975.

——, *Kunst im Lichte der Mysterienweisheit*, GA 275, Dornach 1966. Also in English as: *Art as Seen in the Light of Mystery Wisdom*.

——, *Kunst und Kunsterkenntnis*, GA 271, Dornach 3 ed 1985.

——, *Man as a Symphony of the Creative Word*, Steiner Press, London 1979.

——, *Materialism and the Task of Anthroposophy*, Anthroposophic Press, New York 1987.

——, *Meditative Betrachtungen und Anleitungen zur Vertiefung der Heilkunst*, GA 316, Dornach 2 ed 1980.

——, *Mein Lebensgang*, GA 28, Dornach 7 ed 1962. Also in English as: *The Course of My Life*.

——, *Der Mensch als Zusammenklang des schaffenden, bildenden und gestaltenden Weltenwortes*, GA 230, Dornach 5 ed 1978. Also in English as: *Man as a Symphony of the Creative Word*.

——, *Die Methodik des Lehrens und die Lebensbedingungen des Erziehens*, GA 308, Dornach 5 ed 1986. Also in English as: *The Essentials of Education*.

——, *Methodische Grundlagen der Anthroposophie*, GA 30, Dornach 1961.

——, *Mysterienstätten des Mittelalters*, GA 233a, Dornach 4 ed 1980. Also in English as: *Rosicrucianism and Modern Initiation*.

——, *Mythen und Sagen. Okkulte Zeichen und Symbole*, GA 101, Dornach 1987.

——, *Occult Science — An Outline*, Steiner Press, London 1969.

——, *Pastoral Medicine*, Anthroposophic Press, New York 1987.

——, *Pastoral-Medizinischer Kurs*, GA 318, Dornach 2 ed 1973. Also in English as: *Pastoral Medicine*.

——, *Perspektiven der Menschheitsentwicklung*, GA 204, Dornach 1979. Also in English as: *Materialism and the Task of Anthroposophy*.

——, *Die Philosophie der Freiheit*, GA 4, Dornach 14 ed 1978. Also in English as: *The Philosophy of Freedom.* and *A Philosophy of Spiritual Activity*.

——, *Philosophie und Anthroposophie*, collected essays 1904–18, GA 35, Dornach 1965.

——, *The Philosophy of Freedom: A Philosophy of Spiritual Activity*, Steiner Press, London 1989.

——, *The Philosophy of Spiritual Activity: a Philosophy of Freedom,* Steiner Press, Bristol 1992.

——, *Die Rätsel der Philosophie,* GA 18, Dornach 9 ed 1985. Also in English as: *The Riddles of Philosophy.*

——, *The Renewal of Education through the Science of the Spirit,* Kolisko Archive Publications, Bournemouth 1981.

——, *The Riddles of Philosophy,* Anthroposophic Press, New York 1973.

——, *Rosicrucianism and Modern Initiation,* Steiner Press, London 1982.

——, *Rudiments of Esotericism,* Steiner Press, London 1982.

——, *Das Sonnenmysterium,* GA 211, Dornach 1963.

——, *The Spiritual Guidance of Man and Humanity,* Anthroposophic Press, New York 1983.

——, *Study of Man, General Education Course.* Steiner Press, London 1981.

——, *A Theory of Knowledge Implicit in Goethe's World Conception,* Anthroposophic Press, New York 1985.

——, *Von Seelenrätseln,* GA 21, Dornach 4 ed, 1960. Also in English as: *The Case for Anthroposophy.*

——, *Welt- und Lebensanschauungen des 19. Jahrhunderts* appeared in 1900/1901 and in an expanded new edition in 1914 as *Rätsel der Philosophie.* English translation: *The Riddles of Philosophy.*

——, *Weltenwunder, Seelenprüfungen und Geistesoffenbarungen,* Dornach 5 ed 1977, GA 129. Also in English as: *Wonders of the World.*

——, *Das Wesen des Musikalischen und das Tonerleben im Menschen,* GA 283, Dornach 3 ed 1981. Also in English as: *The Inner Nature of Music and the Experience of Tone.*

——, *Wonders of the World,* Steiner Press, London 1988.

Steiner, Rudolf, and Marie Steiner-von Sivers, *Correspondence and Documents,* Steiner Press, London 1988.

Stratz, C.H., *Der Körper des Kindes und seine Pflege,* Stuttgart 12 ed 1941.

Toldt-Hochstetter, *Anatomischer Atlas,* München 27 ed 1979.

Uhde, Jürgen, *Beethovens Klaviermusik,* Vol.1

Wachsmuth, G., *Die ätherischen Bildekräfte im Kosmos, Erde und Mensch,* Philosophisch-Anthroposophischer Verlag, Dornach 2 ed 1926.

Zeylmans van Emmichoven, F.W., *Die menschliche Seele. Einführung in die Kenntnis des Wesens, der Tätigkeit und der Entwicklung der Seele,* Verlag Die Pforte, Basel 2 ed 1979.

Zuckerkandl, Viktor, *Die Wirklichkeit der Musik,* Rhein Verlag, Zurich, 1963.

Index